TEN

Milton Meltzer

illustrated by Bethanne Andersen

DUTTON CHILDREN'S BOOKS   NEW YORK

QUEENS

Portraits of
WOMEN *of* POWER

Text copyright © 1998 by Milton Meltzer

Illustrations copyright © 1998 by Bethanne Andersen

All rights reserved.

CIP Data is available.

Published in the United States by Dutton Children's Books,

a member of Penguin Putnam Inc.

375 Hudson Street, New York, New York 10014

Designed by Sara Reynolds

Maps by Richard Amari

Printed in Italy

First Edition

1 2 3 4 5 6 7 8 9 10

ISBN 0-525-45643-0

For Eleanor Roosevelt—
never a queen,
but the greatest First Lady

M. M.

For Steven,
new and old school

B. A. A.

Contents

*W*hy this book about the ten queens?

These are not women who were called queens because they happened to marry a king and had little or nothing to say about ruling the country.

These ten were women of power. Most ruled in their own right, by themselves. Or if they sat on thrones beside kings, they had as much or more to say about governing than their husbands.

Each held a throne in a time when all power was vested in the monarch. The "divine right of kings"—you've heard about that. Monarchs believed that God had chosen them to rule. That was interpreted to mean the king or queen could do no wrong. For how could God have been mistaken? Some monarchs felt it gave them license to do whatever pleased them, with no concern for how their decisions affected the people. They could be as arrogant, as selfish, as cruel as they liked. The only restriction on their behavior was fear of a popular uprising if they went too far.

Other monarchs—whether by nature, upbringing, religious belief, or common humanity—did their best to rule benevolently, to help improve the lives of their subjects. Without, of course, handing over to the people any of their power. During most of the centuries covered in this book, democracy was an idea whose time had not yet come.

Monarchs, judged by their behavior on the throne, might be considered by us now as good or evil. Some were both good and evil. That is, at times they ruled on behalf of their subjects, and at other times they worked against the common good. Like most people everywhere, at whatever time, they were a mixture of elements: complex, contradictory, unpredictable.

So the queens in this book were not chosen because they were heroines or saints. No, but because they were women who held power in their own hands and used it. Most had qualities to be wished for in any person, male or female: intellect, courage, independence.

You will see as you read about these lives that certain aspects of their stories echo familiarly. When a woman becomes powerful—in politics or other spheres of life—she inspires great resentment and even hatred. Many obviously false stories circulate about her. As time passes, it becomes hard to tell what is false and what is true.

The traditional belief was that the subjugation of women was part of the divine order. Women were born inferior to men, it was said. If a woman took the leading role in any enterprise, however small or large, it was felt to be unnatural. Throughout the ages, women who achieved something were regarded as unfeminine, unwomanly. So you can imagine how women such as Elizabeth I of England or Catherine the Great of Russia, who held their own as rulers most successfully, were seen in a world previously dominated by men.

For these brief profiles in power, my task was to illuminate how these queens came to power, and what they did with power when it was in their hands.

The index will be useful to readers who wish to compare various aspects of the queens' lives.

The note on sources indicates the problems of research for this kind of book.

Ten Queens

Esther

One of the earliest queens known to us is Esther, the Jewish wife of King Ahasuerus of Persia. Her story is found in the Old Testament, in the Book of Esther. Jews around the world celebrate her heroism every year with the Feast of Purim, an immensely popular folk festival held in early spring. In the Bible, Esther foils the plot of the king's prime minister, Haman, to wipe out all the Jews of the empire.

How did that plot come about? The tale takes place in the 5th century B.C. Ahasuerus is known in history as Xerxes I, king of the Persian empire. He ruled over vast territories, including parts of Asia, Egypt, and Greece. He was married to Queen Vashti, whose beauty he was proud of. One day while feasting in the palace together with leading men of his empire, he ordered the servants to bring the queen to him so that he could show off her beauty to the guests.

Vashti, probably unwilling to be demeaned as a toy, refused to come. The king was furious. Don't let her get away with this! urged his chief counselors. She's only encouraging other wives to disobey their husbands!

You're right, said the king, and he set Vashti aside forever. I want a worthier woman as queen, he said. Fetch me beautiful maidens from all my provinces so that I can choose the most beautiful to be my new queen.

Esther and the king

Many young women were chosen to come to Susa, the Persian capital. For a year they were given special beauty treatments with oils and spices, and then they were brought to the king. But to not one of them was he attracted.

It happened that on the king's staff there was a wise and devout man called Mordecai. He was one of the Jews exiled from Jerusalem when enemies of his people conquered the city. He had a lovely adopted daughter, an orphaned cousin of his named Esther. Now she was brought to the palace, and when the king saw her, he fell in love immediately. He set the royal crown on her head and made her queen.

The king did not know Esther was Jewish. On the advice of Mordecai, she never mentioned it. Why not? It doesn't seem that she and Mordecai were trying to hide from anti-Semitism in the modern sense. It's very likely that King Ahasuerus, like most Persian rulers, was more or less tolerant of the various religions and peoples within his empire.

It was common in those times—and it still is!—for a ruler's favorite to be rewarded with special privileges for his or her relatives. Yet Esther did not seek such

benefits for her people. Maybe it was a case of inspired foresight and awareness of the sorrows to come.

One day Mordecai overheard two counselors of Ahasuerus plotting to assassinate the king. He asked Esther to warn her husband. She did, and the conspirators were arrested and executed.

Soon afterward, the king chose a man named Haman to be his prime minister. Now, palace officials were expected to bow down before the prime minister whenever they encountered him. And so they did. But not Mordecai. A proud man, he would not lower himself to do that. He felt inferior to no one. Haman was enraged by his refusal. A Jew, he growled, an outsider, like all his people. As time went on, Haman's anger turned to hatred. One day he went to the king and passionately denounced the empire's Jews: "There is a certain people scattered abroad and dispersed among the peoples in all the provinces of your kingdom; their laws are different from those of other people, and they do not keep the king's laws, so that it is not in the king's profit to tolerate them."

Now, the Persian empire, like other empires in ancient times, held many nations within its bounds. The rulers usually made no attempt to force a religion on nations, or to interfere too much in their daily lives. They had learned it was better that way. To do otherwise might cause chaos and revolts. So they appointed leading people in each province to govern the inhabitants, subject only to general policy—and of course taxation!—set by the capital. A peaceful empire meant continuing profits.

Apparently the king trusted Haman, and accepted his anti-Jewish propaganda. To tip the balance even more against the Jews, Haman said he would pay a large sum into the royal treasury if the king would let him decide what to do about the Jews. No, I don't want the money, the king said, but you have my permission to do as you see fit about the Jews. And he gave Haman his signet ring, needed to authorize any royal decree the prime minister might draw up.

Haman decided to rid the empire of all the Jews. He had magicians cast a sacred lot (called a *pur*—hence Purim) to select the right day to carry out his evil plan. Then he sent messengers to the leaders of all the provinces, ordering them on the appointed day to have the local Jews killed and their property seized.

Haman's plot could not be kept secret. When word of their coming fate leaked out, the Jews were horrified. They fasted, prayed, and tore their clothes in mourning.

Mordecai came to Esther and showed her a copy of Haman's orders. Go to the king, he said, and do all you can to get him to save our people!

Esther figured out how best to accomplish this. She fasted for three days, to pray for the success of her mission, and then, dressed in her queenly robes, went to the king. She invited him to come dine with her in her wing of the palace, and to bring Haman with him. This the king did. After the meal, Esther asked the king and Haman to come again the next day.

Haman was delighted by this extraordinary honor. But on his way home, he happened to see Mordecai in the palace square. His anger boiled up, and he ordered that a gallows be built on the square. He meant to ask the king the next day to have Mordecai, the first victim of his pogrom, hanged there.

That night, after the meal, the king had trouble sleeping. Thinking it might help him fall asleep, he called for the court records to be read to him, and came across an entry reporting that it was Mordecai who had detected the plot to assassinate the king. But he found no record that Mordecai had been rewarded for saving his life.

So when Haman came in to see him the next morning, the king asked him, "What shall be done to the man whom the king delights to honor?" Thinking that the king was referring to him, Haman was overjoyed. Dress such a man in royal robes, he advised. Place him upon the king's horse, and let a royal official lead him through the streets of the capital. Imagine Haman's shocked reaction when the king said all right, see that exactly this is done for Mordecai!

That evening, when the king and Haman joined Esther for the second banquet, she seemed depressed. What's the matter, the king asked, is something upsetting you?

This was a crucial moment for Esther, the time when she must reveal herself as a Jew and risk everything. She had become a queen, reaching the height of ambition and achievement that a woman in those days could hope for. If she revealed her identity, she might lose her exalted position, and life itself, at one stroke. On the other hand, if she safeguarded her position and remained silent,

Esther confronts Haman

she would be a traitor to her faith and her people, and would have to live out the rest of her life in that knowledge.

She poured out the truth: My people are to be destroyed, to be slain, to be annihilated! And you, she said, pointing at the terrified Haman, you are the one who has organized this mass murder! Save us, she pleaded with the king, save my life and the lives of all my people!

So shocked was the king that he rushed out into the garden. Haman flung himself down on a couch next to Esther and begged her to save his life. At that moment the king returned, and seeing Haman next to the queen, he cried out,

Esther

"Will he even assault the queen in my presence, in my own house?" He called for guards to seize Haman, and ordered that he be hanged on the gallows that Haman himself had prepared for Mordecai.

The king confiscated Haman's house and possessions and gave them to Esther. He appointed Mordecai prime minister in Haman's place. Mordecai went out of the palace dressed in royal robes of blue and white, with a great golden crown and a purple mantle of fine linen, and the whole city shouted and rejoiced.

But what about Haman's murderous decree? There were plenty of people in the provinces ready to carry it out. Esther begged the king to have Haman's decree cancelled. This was impossible, for Persian law made an edict of the ruler irrevocable even by the ruler himself. Instead, Mordecai was told to send out another decree, giving Jews the right to arm themselves in self-defense. It was rushed on fast horses and camels to all the provinces of the empire.

On the day Haman had set for the destruction, the Jews faced their enemies and killed them.

According to the Book of Esther, the Feast of Purim was established by Esther and Mordecai to celebrate the Jews' deliverance from persecution.

Book of Esther

The story of Esther, the savior of her people as told in the Bible, is legendary. Historians have found no documentary evidence as to what historical events may have provided the basis for the story. The Book of Esther itself seems to have been composed hundreds of years later than the period of the reign of Xerxes, who died in 465 B.C. It is thought, however, that the origin of the Purim festival may date back to the sixth century B.C., when the Jews went into exile in Babylon.

The Book of Esther asserts that the Jews killed 75,000 of their enemies.

"Hardly anyone outside of Orthodox Jewry believes this ever happened," says Arthur Waskow, a scholar of Jewish history. "Almost everyone takes this tale . . . as a fantasy. The dream of the powerless that once, just once, they could fight back and destroy everyone who ever sneered at them."

Purim

Esther

Cleopatra

69 B.C. – 30 B.C.

The most famous woman in Roman history was not a Roman. Cleopatra—that was her name—was queen of Egypt. Then was she an Egyptian? No, she was a Greek. Sounds like a muddle. But let's try to straighten it out by looking at some facts. These facts are not easy to come by. Yet scarcity of information has not stopped people from creating a great many poems, plays, novels, biographies, and movies about Cleopatra.

In one such work you are told that Cleopatra is the wickedest woman in history. In others she is a sexual glutton. Or a faithful, tender lover who died for her man. Or she is a public benefactor or a selfish tyrant or a child who never grew up or a beauty made into a hag by constant sinning.

Not much of what such works tell us is based on hard fact. One reason is that Cleopatra lived a very long time ago. Almost two thousand years have passed since she died in 30 B.C. It is difficult to know the details of what really happened back then. Scanty evidence survives from ancient history. It consists of the find-ings of archeologists; of inscriptions on monuments, temples, and tombs; of portraits on coins and medals.

Then there are the writings of the period, deciphered from parchments that have endured. (It would be a long time before printing would be invented.) These include letters, memoirs, speeches, and the accounts of ancient historians, usually written decades or even centuries after the leading personalities had gone to their graves.

historical evidence

But the evidence we do have indicates that Cleopatra was a woman of powerful ambition. She had the keen intelligence, the charm, and the political savvy to make a great mark on the life of her time. To be an effective ruler of a nation or an empire you must have such qualities. Think of it as being the CEO (chief executive officer) of a vast business concern. You must have specific goals in mind; you must make plans to achieve those goals; you must recruit able managers; you must create messages to express your program and win the loyalty and support of your people. And you need always to maintain an air of confident authority. People must believe that you know what you're doing and how to go about getting the job done.

Cleopatra was born in 69 B.C., the third daughter of Ptolemy XII, king of Egypt. She would be the last Greek ruler of Egypt in a dynasty that began long ago when Egypt was conquered by Alexander the Great. That young warrior came from Macedonia, a country in northern Greece. He stayed in Egypt long enough to be installed as pharaoh (the title of its kings). He made Egypt a province of the new Macedonian empire. To honor himself he founded a city on Egypt's Mediterranean coast and named it Alexandria.

Upon Alexander's death, his huge empire cracked and fell into separate states.

He had been an absolute monarch: no one else had any say in the important decisions. So when one of his generals, named Ptolemy, took control of Egypt, that was how he too ruled. Under the dynasty Ptolemy founded, Egypt flourished. The regime made Greek the official language, and the art of the Greek world reshaped the age-old Egyptian art. Egypt's army was established as an efficient fighting machine. But in religion the Ptolemies were careful not to offend the Egyptians. They cultivated the principal deities of the Egyptian pantheon and constructed great temples honoring them. The Ptolemies adopted the Egyptian royal titles and such Egyptian customs as brother-sister marriage of rulers and the identification of rulers with gods. They developed commerce, built new ports, and extended contacts with Asia and the classical lands of Rome and Greece. They became great patrons of the arts and learning and founded a great library at Alexandria.

Over the centuries of their rule, the Ptolemies amassed a vast royal treasury by exploiting the Egyptians. Wealth flowed away from the peasant producers and into royal hands. The gap between rich and poor became wider in Egypt than in most of the Greco-Roman world.

But wealthy as the Ptolemies were, they ruled only by permission of Rome, a much greater power. Still, the Ptolemies were never content to limit their rule to Egypt. They sought to conquer great tracts of territory far beyond their borders.

It was no different for the Romans, great empire builders themselves. Around the time of Cleopatra, it's estimated, the total area of the Roman empire was about 1,250,000 square miles, and the population, perhaps 60 million. (That is the population of Italy today.) Everyone except the citizens who lived mostly in Rome itself, or close by, was a subject, ruled by the "Roman people." These subjects lived in provinces or colonies, just as America and India were British colonies before they won their independence.

The Romans had long had their eye on Egypt's lands and wealth. At the time of Cleopatra's birth, Egypt seemed ripe for the picking. Fearful of a Roman takeover, Cleopatra's father, Ptolemy XII, cozied up to the empire's leaders. He knew his Egypt was now a second-rank state. Why not seek the protection of the world's great superpower? So he offered Rome a deal. At that time Rome was ruled by a triumvirate—three men—Julius Caesar, Pompey, and Crassus, all powerful generals. If you declare publicly that you recognize my right to the Egyptian throne, Ptolemy said, I'll pay you for it. Done, said the three, promptly proclaiming him a "friend and ally of the Roman people." Of course they made him pay dearly.

Julius Caesar

Where would Ptolemy get the money demanded? He couldn't increase the taxation of his subjects; they were angry with him as it was. He borrowed the money from a Roman moneylender. Within two years, the Egyptians were plotting against their king, and Ptolemy fled to Rome for safety, taking twelve-year-old Cleopatra with him. With Ptolemy gone, his eldest daughter seized the throne. In Rome, Ptolemy persuaded a general to restore him to the throne—in return for lots of cash, of course. But before the Roman soldiers reached Egypt, that daughter was dead, probably murdered by her father's friends.

Meanwhile, Ptolemy's second daughter had seized power. But when the

Roman troops placed Ptolemy back on his throne, he promptly had that daughter executed. In those times, such ruthless behavior was common. In 51 B.C., Ptolemy XII died. In his will, he named Cleopatra and his son, Ptolemy XIII, his joint heirs. She was eighteen, he was ten.

What was Cleopatra, now the teenage queen, like? No description of her from the time survives. Writing about a hundred years later, the Greek historian Plutarch said she was not a beauty. She had a fairly dark complexion, which people said was due to the mixed blood of the Macedonians. In portraits of her on coins, she has a lively expression, a sensitive mouth, a strong chin, a wide forehead, liquid eyes, and a prominent nose. Her voice, said Plutarch, "was like an instrument of many strings," and her charm made her delightful company.

But beneath the beguiling manner was substance. Her father had arranged for her to learn Egyptian as well as Greek, and she had acquired at least six other languages of the Middle East and Africa. From her father too she gained a love of music.

These centuries before the beginnings of Christianity were an age of ruler-worship. Kings, who had unlimited power to save or destroy, were regarded as more than human. The Egyptian pharaohs had been god kings for eons, and the Greek Ptolemies too gave themselves such titles as "Our Lord, the King." So Cleopatra was a goddess even before she ascended the throne. This was more than self-flattery. It was a deliberate policy meant to focus the people's feelings of loyalty and patriotism upon the ruler. Young as she was, Cleopatra understood that psychology. She would always make use of it to fulfill her supreme hope of continuing the dynasty of Ptolemies as an independent power.

The first two years of Cleopatra's reign didn't go well. The advisers to her little brother, who shared the throne with her, disliked Cleopatra and worked against her. It was bad luck when the Nile failed to rise high enough to flood the lands alongside the river and ensure a good harvest of the crops. Food shortage caused popular discontent. Rather than pay taxes, poor peasants deserted their villages.

In her handling of foreign affairs Cleopatra met with still more trouble. Believing her father's ties with the Romans made sense, she ordered troops to help the Roman governor of Syria against the Parthians, famous horsemen and archers of an Asian land. The Egyptian soldiers refused to go, saying Rome's problems were no concerns of theirs. Fearing a popular uprising, Cleopatra fled Alexandria and went to Rome. That left her brother's supporters in control of the government.

Meanwhile, in Rome, civil war had broken out between Caesar and Pompey. Beaten in battle, Pompey fled to Egypt, pursued by Caesar. As Pompey landed in Alexandria, he was murdered. Caesar entered the city a few days later, intending to plunder Egypt's riches to pay the expenses of the civil war.

The twenty-one-year-old Cleopatra arrived back in Alexandria soon after, and set out to captivate the great Caesar. She hoped to win his powerful aid to maintain herself in office. She rolled herself up in a rug and had herself smuggled past her brother's guards and into Caesar's quarters in the royal palace. The young queen's trick amused and delighted Caesar, the aging veteran of many love affairs as well as wars. This irresistible young woman was imperious, courageous, and ambitious as he was.

The two became lovers. Caesar took her part in the power struggle between Cleopatra and her brother's faction. To put a stop to their quarrels, Caesar decreed that brother and sister should rule jointly. Nevertheless, fighting broke out. Caesar's troops fought and won for Cleopatra; her brother was found drowned in the Nile. A victim of war? Or murder?

It would have been easy for Caesar to annex Egypt. Perhaps out of loyalty to Cleopatra, he didn't. Besides, it was easier to obtain some of the country's wealth by accepting its money and keeping Cleopatra on the throne. He had her married to her youngest brother, then about twelve, and proclaimed them joint rulers of Egypt. This observed the Ptolemaic custom of brother-sister marriage of rulers, but it was an empty gesture. For the boy had no strong faction behind him, which left Cleopatra, in effect, to rule alone.

Caesar then sailed away from Egypt, leaving three of his legions behind to support Cleopatra. By the time he departed, Cleopatra was pregnant.

For the next year foreign wars kept Caesar busy. When he returned to Rome in the fall of 46 B.C., there was Cleopatra to welcome him. Not alone, but with her brother-king husband and her baby. She had named the child Ptolemy Caesar (nicknamed Caesarion) to let the world know who his famous father was. Caesar, however, never publicly admitted he was the father.

Cleopatra stayed in Rome for a year and a half, a guest in Caesar's royal palace, while her ministers, or cabinet, took care of business in Egypt. She maintained a splendid court in Rome. But she did more than entertain royally. Under her influence, and with the advice of experts she brought with her, Caesar introduced some innovations in Rome. One was the reform of the calendar to introduce a solar year of 365 days, with an extra day every four years (leap year). Both the Roman empire and the modern world adopted it. Again, following Egypt's example, Caesar also constructed canals to improve transport and extended learning by building great public libraries, modeled on the most famous one in the world at Alexandria.

In tribute to Cleopatra, Caesar placed a gilt-bronze statue of her in a public forum. It did not signify that he was going to marry her, for he already had a wife, Calpurnia. Bigamy was forbidden by Roman law, and so was marriage to a foreigner.

Cleopatra's statue

Officially Cleopatra was in Rome to negotiate a treaty of alliance and friendship with her country. At this time Rome was completely dominated by Caesar. He was dictator in all but name, and he saw to it that the treaty was signed. Caesar's open contempt for the conservative Roman nobility and his desire to rule without their interference led to his downfall. On the Ides of March, in 44 B.C., a band of conspirators, led by Brutus and Cassius, assassinated him.

Cleopatra had lost her patron, lover, and friend. When Caesar's will was read two days later, neither Cleopatra nor Caesarion was mentioned. Cleopatra decided to leave Rome and return to Egypt with her brother-king. A few months later, that youngster was dead. Some people suspected that she had him killed.

A widow again, she appointed her child, Caesarion, to share her throne. Ever hungry for more power, she claimed that the boy was the true heir of Caesar, believing this gave the two of them the right to govern the entire world of the Mediterranean. In reality, of course, she was the sole ruler.

Now in her mid-twenties, Cleopatra gave all her energy to governing her country. Although we cannot be sure of the facts, many accounts have paid tribute to Cleopatra for her scholarship and philanthropy. She was believed to be the author of works on weights and measures, on coinage, on gynecology, and on alchemy. An Arab author wrote that she was well informed on the sciences, studied philosophy, and counted many scholars among her intimate friends. She created a public works department and commissioned many of the great engineering projects that advanced Egypt's economy and prosperity.

After Caesar's death, a struggle for power took place among the leading men of Rome. It ended with the victory of two of them: Octavian, Caesar's nineteen-year-old adopted son; and Antony, forty, a talented military commander and one

Cleopatra's barge

of Rome's leading political figures. The two men split the empire between them, with Octavian taking western Europe and Antony, the Roman East.

Antony, who was married to Fulvia, an intelligent and ambitious woman, decided to carry out Caesar's intention to invade the Parthian empire (roughly the territory of today's Iran and Iraq). Thus he could claim Caesar's heritage as champion of all the Romans. But he needed lots of money for such an expedition. Like so many before him, he turned to Egypt for financial and military help.

Instead of going to Alexandria, Antony summoned Cleopatra to meet him in Tarsus, his headquarters in Asia Minor, so they could work out an alliance against the Parthians. She seized the opportunity to take advantage of his widely known weakness for women. With Caesar gone, she needed a new partner to strengthen her rule over Egypt, and perhaps to extend it. She kept putting off the trip, whetting his curiosity all the more. Finally she set out, loaded with gifts to display Egypt's wealth. She entered Tarsus by sailing up the River Cydnus in a luxurious state barge. In his play *Antony and Cleopatra*, Shakespeare immortalized the vessel.

C l e o p a t r a

19

Constructed of cedar and cypress, it was 300 feet long, with its decks designed as arcaded courts. Musicians, clowns, a procession of women bearing flowers, and priests in their colorful robes crowded down to the river to meet the woman whose skill in what we today call public relations had made people believe she was a goddess with power even greater than that of an earthly queen. As her boat moved to the bank, wrote Plutarch,

> *Her rowers caressed the water with oars of silver which dipped to the music of the flute, accompanied by pipes and lutes. . . . Instead of a crew the barge was lined with the most beautiful of her waiting women attired as Nereids and Graces, some at the rudders, others at the tackles of the sails, and all the while an indescribably rich perfume, exhaled from innumerable censers, was wafted from the vessel to the river banks.*

Like Caesar, Antony was captivated by Cleopatra, and she by this famously attractive man. He forgot about his wife, who had stayed in Rome to protect her husband's interests from any encroachment by the young Octavian. It appears from the historical record that Cleopatra was much smarter and more strong-willed than Antony. Where physical courage was demanded, Antony was always up to the mark, but he was often the victim of his appetites for love and luxury. Cleopatra was easily able to beguile him into postponing the Parthian campaign and returning to Alexandria with her.

Cleopatra saw Antony as the means to extend Egypt's domain in the East. She could supply the funds and the political skills while he could supply Roman legions. The two of them wanted to meld the power and the culture of Rome and the East into one great empire.

While Antony lingered in Egypt, the Parthians in 40 B.C. began to invade Rome's eastern territory. Antony left for the battlefront only to learn on the way that his wife and brother had led a revolt against Octavian that had been crushed, with Fulvia dying soon after. With the situation so grave, Antony went to Italy to meet with Octavian. Octavian proposed they forget their differences and cement an alliance with a marriage between Antony and Octavian's sister Octavia.

Cleopatra had been terribly disappointed when the news of Fulvia's death had not made Antony return to Egypt. That same year of 40 B.C. she had given birth to twins, a boy and a girl fathered by Antony. Now she was doubly upset to hear that Antony had married Octavia, who was not only younger than she, but also beautiful and intelligent.

Antony

In the winter of 39 B.C., Antony and Octavia moved to the Greek city of Athens, making it the capital of his eastern empire. Late in that year Octavia bore him a daughter. Still, Antony could not forget Cleopatra nor give up the promise of military glory fighting for a greater empire. In 37 B.C. he rejoined Cleopatra, planning to use Egypt's treasury for his campaign to add Parthia to his eastern realm.

In 36 B.C. Antony and Cleopatra seem to have gone through some sort of marriage ceremony just before the birth of another child, a boy. Then Antony took off for his much-postponed campaign against Parthia.

For the next few years Antony carried on wars that proved to be total disasters or brought only short-lived success. Everyone grew sick of the bloodshed and destruction and yearned for peace. To calm the public, Octavian declared that civil wars were over. Antony, he said, was now just a private citizen, serving that alien queen Cleopatra. This may have been a hint to Antony and his Roman followers that if they wanted to switch sides, they would be welcomed. But when Antony showed he had no intention of doing that, Octavian declared war—not on Antony, but on Cleopatra. She and Antony gathered their forces to fight Octavian. On September 2, 31 B.C. they were defeated in the naval battle of Actium off the western coast of Greece. Although three quarters of their fleet was captured or destroyed, Antony and Cleopatra managed to evade capture.

Octavian had come out on top in the battle for supremacy. The soldiers who had fought for him now demanded money and land for their service. To satisfy them he needed to take over the great treasure of Egypt still in Cleopatra's hands.

As he moved his forces toward Egypt, the supporters of Antony and Cleopatra changed sides. They knew who the winner would be. Both Cleopatra and

Cleopatra

These lines describing Cleopatra's entry into Tarsus to meet Antony are from Shakespeare's play Antony and Cleopatra, *Act II, Scene ii. Shakespeare drew most of the details from his main source for the play, Plutarch's life of Antony.*

The barge she sat in, like a burnish'd throne,

Burn'd on the water; the poop was beaten gold,

Purple the sails, and so perfumed that

The winds were love-sick with them; the oars were silver,

Which to the tune of flutes kept stroke, and made

The water which they beat to follow faster,

As amorous of their strokes. For her own person

It beggar'd all description; she did lie

In her pavilion—cloth-of-gold of tissue—

O'er-picturing that Venus where we see

The fancy outwork nature; on each side her

Stood pretty-dimpled boys, like smiling Cupids,

With divers-colour'd fans, whose wind did seem

To glow the delicate cheeks which they did cool,

And what they undid did. . . .

                          At the helm

A seeming mermaid steers; the silken tackle

Swell with the touches of those flower-soft hands,

That yarely frame the office. From the barge

A strange invisible perfume hits the sense

Of the adjacent wharfs. The city cast

Her people out upon her; and Antony,

Enthron'd i' th' market-place, did sit alone,

Whistling to the air: which, but for vacancy,

Had gone to gaze on Cleopatra too,

And made a gap in nature.

Antony sent messages to Octavian offering to quit and retire if he would spare them. He did not reply. With both the Egyptian fleet and army deserting to Octavian, he entered Alexandria without a fight. Cleopatra hid in the mausoleum she had built for herself and where she stored Egypt's treasure. When a false rumor that Cleopatra had committed suicide reached Antony, he plunged his sword into his body. As he lay dying, he was carried into Cleopatra's hiding place. There he died in her arms.

Octavian sent his men into the mausoleum to take Cleopatra alive and to prevent her setting fire to her treasure. Captured, she was brought to the palace. She believed Octavian meant to carry her and her children to Rome to display them in his triumphal parade. Rather than be dragged through the streets of the city where she had once been honored as a queen, she killed herself. According to the legend concerning her death, she poisoned herself with the bite of an asp.

Octavian had her buried beside Antony in her mausoleum. He promised the Egyptians he would be lenient with them. But he killed Caesarion, the reputed son of Julius Caesar and a potential rival one day for Octavian's throne. The children of Antony and Cleopatra he left unharmed.

The death of Cleopatra brought to an end her great ambition—to continue the dynasty of the Ptolemies as an independent power. Egypt was annexed to the Roman empire. Octavian, now calling himself Caesar Augustus, would rule over his vast domain for another forty-five years.

Boudicca

A. D. circa 28 – 62

I n the days of their vast and flourishing empire, the Romans were so sure of themselves that they did not think it possible any of their colonies could revolt successfully. For some five hundred years—from shortly before the birth of Christ to the late 400's A.D.—Roman rulers would control most of Europe, North Africa, the Middle East, and Asia as far as the Caspian and the Black seas. Imagine their horror when a rebel army of Britons revolted, capturing three cities and wiping out their inhabitants. And "moreover," wrote the Roman historian Dio Cassius, "all this ruin was brought upon [them] by a woman, a fact which in itself caused them the greatest shame."

That woman was Boudicca. Her power to command became legendary. What did she look like? Dio gives us this description: She was very tall, the glance of her eye most fierce, and her voice harsh. A great mass of the reddest hair fell down to her hips. Around her neck was a large golden necklace, and she always

wore a tunic of many colors, over which she fastened a thick cloak with a brooch. Her appearance was terrifying.

Boudicca's people, called the Iceni, were one of the many tribes descended from the Celts scattered throughout Britain. The Celts flourished in western Europe for over a thousand years—from the early Iron Age to the establishment of Christianity. All Celts spoke dialects of a common language. Like most early peoples, they were essentially illiterate. The spoken word was supreme, and they relied on oral traditions to preserve their ways of life.

Most Celts were tall, fair-skinned, blond, and blue-eyed. Both men and women wore colored tunics and cloaks. They lived in a "heroic" age, with tribe warring against tribe, more as sport than as grim business. Bravery in battle was supremely prized. They were adventurous but lacked staying power, often quitting the field of combat to plunder. Until the Romans came, the tribes did not live in towns but on the land that they farmed, building hill forts for protection. They harvested and stored grain, and kept pigs, goats, cattle, and sheep. Spinning, weaving, and pottery were home crafts. Most farms were self-supporting, except for metals bought from traders.

Many tribes developed an aristocracy that shared wealth and political power. They rivaled one another in the number of servants, both free and slave. Most of the people, however, probably lived in poverty.

Celtic families were patriarchal. The male head had absolute power over all his household. Yet Celtic women, according to Roman observers, were not only as tall as their men but their equals in courage. And sometimes the power to rule was vested in a woman, such as Boudicca.

Life changed when the Romans invaded Britain. It began with Julius Caesar. He had proved himself as a military commander in conquering parts of the continent such as Gaul (France) and Germany. Now he decided to seek further glory and gain by an expedition to Britain, about which little was known.

Although Britain was only across the English Channel, Roman troops were terrified of sailing beyond their known world. It took much persuasion to get them aboard the ships. In August of 55 B.C. the Roman legions landed, routed the opposing Britons, and found several tribal chieftains ready to submit. Caesar himself stayed in Britain only briefly, for problems back in Rome called him home. About a year later he returned to Britain, leading some 25,000 legionaries and 2,000 cavalry, transported on 800 ships. The Romans overcame the resistance of some tribes and were helped by the quick surrender of others. Roman military power and equipment were vastly superior, making opposition almost hopeless. Both sides dickered for peace, and within two months Caesar left on the promise of the Britons paying an annual tribute to Rome.

Although more invasions were rumored, for about a hundred years none came. The Roman victory seemed to have stunned the Britons, for they put up no resistance when Rome set up a chain of garrisons across the conquered territory. As they did throughout their empire, the Romans created an administrative machine to organize and exploit the colony. Trade and cultural contacts with the Continent increased, and the Britons came to see what could be gained by cooperation. Maybe peace was better than tribal warfare. Chieftains who worked with the Roman government gained wealth and influence. The material benefits of the Roman way of life were spreading to ordinary people, too.

In 43 A.D. the emperor Claudius, viewed as a buffoon, tried to solidify his power on the throne by the usual method of conquering new territories. Fresh conflicts among some tribes in Britain gave him the excuse to intervene. Besides, booty was always to be gained through war, and he needed more money to hold the loyalty of the soldiers. So he sent an army into Britain to squelch the disorders and then appeared on the scene himself to take credit for the triumph.

When a new Roman governor, Ostorius, took over in Britain in A.D. 47, hostile tribes from outside the occupied territory attacked. The governor acted swiftly to put down the Britons. But he made a mistake in going further. He disarmed the tribes in the south and east of Britain that had been allowed to keep their weapons under the earlier peace terms. He might have planned to use the region as a jumping-off point to conquer more of Britain. Whatever the governor's motive, the Iceni rebelled. They had long been suffering under the heavy burden of Roman taxation. They bitterly resented the governor's violation of the original agreement. A fierce hatred for Rome took root. Rising in revolt, the Iceni found allies in neighboring tribes. After a hard fight, the Romans defeated the native troops and moved on to conquer tribes in other areas. Now, however, the governor's insensitivity to the feelings of other native tribes brought about the creation of an anti-Rome group among these people.

Little by little the Romans reduced the part of Britain they controlled into a province. To make this new province more secure, Ostorius planted a colony of military veterans at what is now called Colchester. As the first colony, it became the provincial capital, with a temple of Claudius erected in its center. Tribal leaders were allowed kingships over their own immediate areas. It was the traditional Roman way of making native kings the instruments of imposing servitude on the population . . . the process of "Romanization."

The king of the Iceni was Prasutagus. He was married to Boudicca, a woman of royal birth, who bore him two daughters. Around A.D. 59 or 60. Prasutagus died, leaving no male heir. He had entrusted Boudicca with the regency on behalf of their girls. His lands and his personal properties he left jointly to his daughters and the emperor Nero, a stepson of Claudius who succeeded him. That way Prasutagus hoped to win imperial protection for his family's inheritance and to safeguard the tribe's continuation as an ally of Rome, rather than a conquered province.

The Iceni were important to the Romans because their land, just outside the province, was near Colchester, the colony's capital, and they controlled vital water routes inland. Still, Nero decided this was the moment to absorb the Iceni into the Roman province and to ignore Boudicca's rights. We do not like the terms of the king's will, said the Roman officials. They sent men in to seize the king's estate and all his wealth, plundering his kingdom and his household like prizes of war. They tore hereditary lands away from Iceni chiefs. And then, in a savage climax, they flogged Queen Boudicca and raped her two daughters.

Such outrages were enough to make the Iceni revolt by themselves. But other

tribes joined forces with Boudicca and her people. For they too had been milked
of money and deprived of their lands by the greedy Romans.

Gathering her forces, the Warrior Queen headed south for the capital of the
colony at Colchester, which had about 15,000 mostly Roman inhabitants. Tacitus,
a Roman historian of the time of Boudicca, tells us that in preparing her forces
for battle, Boudicca drove around the tribes in a chariot with her daughters. "We
Britons are used to women as commanders in war," she cried. "I am not fighting
for my kingdom and wealth now. I am fighting as an ordinary person for my lost
freedom, my bruised body, and my outraged daughters. Nowadays Roman rapac-
ity does not even spare our bodies. Old people are killed, virgins raped. But the
gods will grant us the vengeance we deserve!"

On the way to Colchester, the rebels killed all the Roman settlers they encountered. Word of their approach reached Colchester ahead of them. But the
warnings of danger went unheeded. Only 200 poorly armed men were on hand
when Boudicca entered the city. Inside was a core of native residents who misled *Boudicca*

the Roman colonists and prevented any serious steps toward the city's defense. Uncertain what to do, the colonists failed to evacuate the noncombatants— women, children, and the aged—even though they had enough warning to send a messenger to Suetonius, the Roman governor, for help. So the city was quickly overrun and destroyed by fire, and the inhabitants slaughtered.

Next Boudicca's forces headed for London. It was then a city of 30,000 colonists and a flourishing mercantile center—a fat prize for a vengeful army of rebels. But before they could reach London, the Britons had to deal with about 2,000 Roman legionaries marching to the rescue. Boudicca demonstrated that her followers were not a leaderless mob. In a carefully planned ambush she cut the Roman infantry to pieces; only the cavalry escaped. The rebels had proved they were more than a match for battle-hardened troops. Meanwhile Suetonius, having heard the dread news, was speeding toward London, but without most of his troops. He mistakenly believed there were many soldiers in the city. He managed to reach London before the queen's men, only to find that the city had no walls, was not fortified, and could not be defended.

He made the hard decision to sacrifice the city to the enemy. Unmoved by prayers and tears of those who begged for help, he gave the order for his cavalry to move out. And, wrote Tacitus, "those who were unfit for war because of their sex, or too aged to go, or too fond of the place to leave, were butchered by the enemy. Never before or since has Britain ever been in a more disturbed and perilous state."

The same massacre took place at Verulamium, a city of 15,000. It looked like Boudicca's revolt might mark the end of Britain's history as part of the Roman empire.

After Suetonius had gathered a force of about 10,000 troops, he decided to engage Boudicca's army at a spot near modern Towcester. He arranged his legionaries in close order in a narrow passageway, with a thick forest behind as protection. He stationed other troops on the flanks and cavalry on both wings. Boudicca's much larger force came to the battleground in loose array. She placed her army's oxcarts, loaded with supplies, women, and children, behind her army, setting them up high on a hill where they could watch the clash of arms.

TEN
QUEENS

The battle was brief. The Romans lured the Britons into attacking the slope, which let the legionaries hurl down upon them two volleys of several thousand javelins—seven feet long with three-foot iron points. That was the end of many of Boudicca's men, who had no body armor to protect them. Then the Romans charged in wedge formation, backed by the cavalry. This attack drove the Britons back on the carts. The battle turned into a massacre as the Romans rushed in, slaughtering the oxen, the troops, and the women and children, who thought to watch their men in another triumph. Tens of thousands of Britons died, and only a tiny fraction of the Romans. Boudicca seems to have escaped from the battlefield. But she died soon after, some said by taking poison, some said due to illness. What happened to her daughters, no one knows.

According to Tacitus, during their revolt the Britons killed something like 70,000 Roman citizens. They "took no prisoners," he said, "sold no captives as slaves and went in for none of the usual trading of war. They wasted no time in getting down to the bloody business of hanging, burning and crucifying. It was as if they feared retribution might catch up with them while their vengeance was only half-complete."

The revolt was an explosion of pent-up hatred. It signified how harsh and corrupt the Roman officials must have been. Suetonius was not going to forget or forgive, even after victory. With fire and sword he methodically laid waste to the territory of all the British tribes that had fought under Boudicca's banner or had remained neutral.

Still, some Britons were ready to fight again. They were desperate, for they had failed to sow crops earlier that year because they expected to capture the Roman military granaries. Hounded by Suetonius, they faced a winter of starvation, even if they survived the governor's punitive attacks.

But a new provincial official sent by Rome understood the reasons for the rebellion. He foresaw the dangerous consequences if Suetonius went on destroying the tribal lands. His reports back to Rome eventually led to the removal of Suetonius from Britain.

The people of Boudicca's region never rebelled again. The Roman occupation of Britain lasted until A.D. 407.

Zenobia

3RD CENTURY A.D.

Less than two hundred years after Boudicca defied the Roman occupiers of her native Britain, another warrior queen daringly declared her independence from Imperial Rome and sought to establish her own united kingdom of the East.

Zenobia was her name, and her capital was Palmyra, an ancient city of Syria, a country that borders the eastern end of the Mediterranean. Zenobia was known for her great physical strength, her beauty, and her brilliance. Little can be said of her history except concerning the five crucial years (A.D. 270–275) when she ruled Palmyra.

Even what has been written of that brief period, all of it by historians of Rome—Zenobia's enemy—varies considerably from one report to another.

Palmyra was a wealthy center of trade and culture, an oasis in the Syrian desert. (The small modern village of Tudmor is now on the site.) The city lay about halfway between the Mediterranean on the west and the Euphrates River

on the east. The road through Palmyra became the natural trade route connecting the Roman world with Mesopotamia and the East. As an oasis near the center of the desert, Palmyra grew into a watering place for caravans of traders and their camels and donkeys.

By the first century B.C., the caravan trade had so enriched Palmyra that the city aroused the envy of its neighbors as well as the greed of Rome. Independent for a long time, Palmyra was forced under Roman control by the emperors of the first century A.D.

Parthia and Persia, already large empires expanding in the East, disliked seeing Rome control the caravan routes. The people of Parthia were famous horsemen and archers who founded the Parthian empire around 250 B.C. Still, in Zenobia's time, the safest caravan route continued to pass through the oasis city, down an avenue lined with 375 Corinthian columns of marble.

The traders came from faraway places: Egypt, the Persian Gulf, India, the Orient. They brought beautiful objects made of gold and silver and ivory. They brought spices and ointments and incense—whatever the East had that the West wanted. The merchants based in Palmyra were organized into companies to increase their profits and provide protection. The families of these merchants lived in fine houses, with couches and floors covered with Persian rugs and plates and

cups studded with precious stones. From the sculpture that has survived we can
see that the women wore embroidered gowns and heavy jewelry, and the men,
wide-flowing trousers and embroidered robes. Mosaics found in the region show
what kinds of food the prosperous people ate: fish, artichokes, pigs' feet, roast
fowl, ham, boiled eggs, and lots of wine.

In Palmyra the written language was Aramaic and the spoken language, Arabic. Aramaic was originally the language of a Semitic people of the desert who
settled in Syria. Zenobia herself was fluent in five tongues—Aramaic, Arabic,
Egyptian, Greek, and Latin. She was apparently of Arabic descent, but there is
no record of who her parents were.

One legend holds that her father was a desert chief with many wives and lots
of sons. He valued daughters only when he could use them to make alliances with
other chiefs. When Zenobia was born, he could see no use for her at that moment. Fearing he would get rid of the child, her mother hid the girl among the
many boys in the sprawling household. She was raised just like them, learning to
shoot arrows, to hunt wild animals, to ride over the desert, to endure any hardship. And to have children only when she wanted them.

She first appears in history as the wife of Odenath, the king of Palmyra. He
was a Romanized Arab, and as was the custom, probably married Zenobia when

Palmyra caravan route

Zenobia

35

she was fourteen or fifteen. They had three sons; the firstborn, the heir to the throne, was named Vaballath.

Rome's bitterest enemy in the East was Sapor I, recently crowned king of the Sassanid Persians. His ambition was to gain world dominion, and he had already named himself king of kings. His first target was Roman Syria. Because the Roman empire was on the verge of collapse, Sapor thought this the right time to strike. In the far west the Britons were rebelling against the Romans occupying their island, and the Goths and other tribes were invading the empire from the north. All this was happening while the powerful Roman legions were murdering one emperor after another, replacing them with men of their own choice. Further weakening the empire was a terrible plague that had been raging for ten years, killing tens of thousands.

The Parthian empire too was in bad shape. By A.D. 230 the Sassanid Persians had defeated the Parthians, using new siege engines to destroy any city that resisted them.

Palmyra under Odenath had increased its prosperity, becoming a center not only for caravan trade but also for the financial operations of the empire. Because Sapor had already attacked several cities of Syria, among them Antioch, which he captured and burned, Zenobia and Odenath feared Palmyra would be next on his list. Meanwhile, Valerian, made emperor of Rome by his legionnaires, had led an army into Syria to defend it from Sapor. But captured by a trick of Sapor's, Valerian was exposed to the mob in the streets. The humiliated seventy-year-old emperor collapsed and died. Sapor had him flayed, his skin stuffed with straw and displayed in a temple as a symbol of Persia's superiority over Rome.

Odenath had been entrusted by the Romans with command over the East, including the Roman legions stationed there. To protect and expand Roman Syria, he led his forces in several successful expeditions against the Persians and the Goths. Then he ravaged Asia Minor in wars that lasted eight years.

He was assisted in his campaigns by Zenobia, reputed to be as able as she was beautiful. At the head of the cavalry of archers rode the king in his chariot, and behind him came Zenobia, on her horse. Both husband and wife wore shining chain armor. One chronicle of their battles maintains that Zenobia was as daring as her husband in combat.

The Romans, happy to see this part of their crumbling empire preserved, gave Odenath the grand title of governor of all the East. But in 267, Odenath was assassinated. Some said his nephew had killed him; others blamed the murder on Zenobia. Whether she was actually guilty, no one knows.

Rome recognized Zenobia's eleven-year-old son, Vaballath, as heir to the throne, and Queen Zenobia as his regent. To help her govern the East, Zenobia

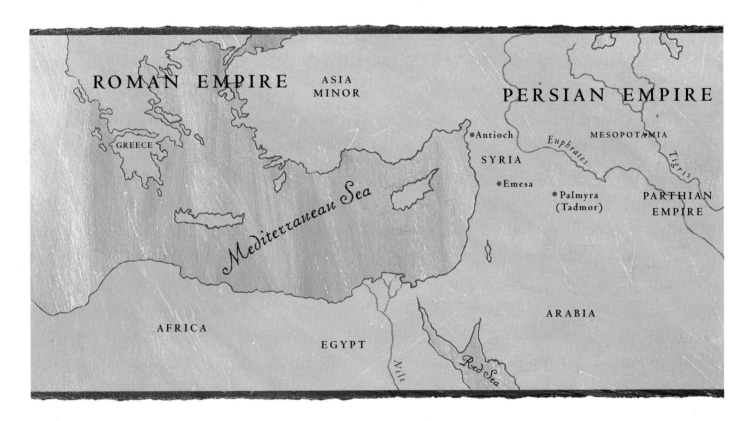

relied on two advisers, the Greek philosopher Longinus and her chief general, Zobdas. Rome's ruler at this time was the emperor Aurelian, a general recently placed in power by his troops. Now in his late fifties, he had had a spectacular military career. As Aurelian hastened to Rome to take control of its corrupt government, Zenobia decided she would end her status as a dependent of Rome. Her ambition was to unite the Empire's eastern dominions—Syria, Egypt, Mesopotamia, and most of Asia Minor—under her leadership.

Zenobia

37

battle at Palmyra

In 269, she sent Zobdas to invade Egypt, one of Rome's richest provinces. After his victory, Zobdas returned to Palmyra with his troops, leaving behind only a tactical force to maintain control.

As word came that Zenobia's campaigns were succeeding, Aurelian marched east to crush the revolt. In a hotly contested battle at Imaae, near Antioch, he defeated Zenobia and Zobdas. The Palmyran forces retreated in good order, but Aurelian pursued them and defeated them again in the decisive battle of Emesa.

Zenobia fled ninety miles east to her desert capital at Palmyra, where she was besieged by Aurelian, who was eager to take the wealthiest city in the eastern domain. Using powerful battering rams, Aurelian assaulted the city walls, but Zenobia's expert archers, shooting arrows down from on high, easily picked off the Roman soldiers. Desert tribes, needing the water from Palmyra's springs, used guerrilla tactics to harry the Romans and cut off their supply of food from the countryside.

Despite the intense heat and his troops' mounting frustration, Aurelian was determined to continue the siege. He wanted Zenobia, and he wanted her alive. Her fabled beauty must have dictated that desire. As one of the chronicles described her:

Her face was dark and of a swarthy hue, her eyes were black and powerful beyond the usual wont, her spirit divinely great, and her beauty incredible. So white were her teeth that many thought she had pearls in place of teeth. Her voice was clear and like that of a man. Her sternness, when necessity demanded, was that of a tyrant, her clemency, that of a great emperor.

As the siege dragged on, some of the Roman soldiers deserted, and Aurelian substituted slaves. They were burned alive as Zenobia's war machines belched liquid fire upon them from her ramparts. But when supplies inside Palmyra began to give out and the water level in its reservoir dropped way down, Zenobia's troops began to sneak out and desert to the Roman camp. Finally, Aurelian decided to end the siege by persuading Zenobia to surrender on his terms. He sent a letter in to her that read in part:

> I bid you surrender, promising that your lives shall be spared, and with the condition that you, Zenobia, together with your children, shall dwell wherever I, acting in accordance with the wish of the most noble Senate, shall appoint a place. Your jewels, your gold, your silver, your silks, your horses, your camels, you shall hand over to the Roman treasury. As for the people of Palmyra, their rights shall be preserved.

Zenobia defied Aurelian's arrogance in demanding she give up as though he were victorious. The emperor ordered the siege renewed. As Palmyra came close to defeat for war-weariness and lack of food, Zenobia thought she saw a way out. She decided to seek military help from Hormizdas, the young king of Persia who had recently taken the throne upon the death of his father, Sapor. If he would ally himself with her, then they might yet prevent the East from falling again under the yoke of the Romans.

She and her son managed to slip out of the city secretly to begin the long and desperate journey to the Persian ruler. Aurelian swiftly learned of her flight and sent mounted soldiers after her. They captured her as she was trying to cross the Euphrates River.

Zenobia was carried in a jolting wagon across the desert of Emesa and ordered to defend her actions before Aurelian. As emperor he acted as both judge and jury, and there was no appeal from an emperor's verdict.

Instead of humbling herself and appealing for mercy, Zenobia boldly said she "desired to become a partner in the royal power." She meant to restore her kingdom to its former glory and to make it a free and independent ally of Rome, not a subject state.

Although she dared behave so insolently before an emperor of Rome, Aurelian did not have her executed. As he wrote in explanation to the Roman Senate, she had performed a valuable service by protecting the eastern frontier of the empire. And perhaps he spared her also because she was a woman, "a beautiful and remarkable woman." His decision infuriated his soldiers, for her revolt had cost them many lives, and they had not been allowed to loot Palmyra. To appease their anger, Aurelian had her chief adviser, Longinus, beheaded.

On the way back to Rome, Aurelian stopped at Antioch with his captives and his booty. There, in the arena, he staged a public show. Wild beasts fought, gladiators slaughtered one another, convicted criminals were executed, and finally in came Zenobia, the great prize. Wearing a Bedouin robe, she entered the ring mounted on a camel. With her foot she guided the camel to Aurelian's box, where the animal went down on its knees.

The next day an iron cage was set up high on a platform in a public square. Zenobia, chained, was held there for three days, exposed to everyone's view. This was a terrible humiliation for a queen. But it was little compared to the fate of other captives of the Roman emperors. Some were condemned to such hard labor in the mines that they quickly died, some had their tongues cut out, some were roasted over slow fires, and many killed themselves to avoid such an end. What Aurelian wanted was to break Zenobia's spirit, not her body.

Released from the cage, Zenobia was put in a curtained oxcart and hauled in Aurelian's cavalcade off to Rome. She would never see her native land again. Behind them, in Palmyra, a revolt broke out. The rebels killed the Roman governor Aurelian had stationed there, as well as the six hundred archers guarding his headquarters. As soon as Aurelian heard of the uprising, he sent in a powerful body of troops to punish the city. Men, women, and children were slaughtered in the streets. Their temple was vandalized, Zenobia's palace was looted, and the city walls were shattered.

In Rome, the Senate voted to grant Aurelian its highest honor, a triumphal entry through the imperial gates in which his legions, his prisoners, and his booty would be displayed. At the head of the long procession was Aurelian, dressed in

a white tunic and a purple cloak, guiding his golden chariot drawn by four antlered stags. Then came wild beasts, hundreds of gladiators, and long lines of prisoners—mostly women and children—representing conquered nations identified by placards held aloft. At last came Zenobia, walking, wearing a long ceremonial robe of heavy purple silk. A light golden collar was around her neck and her arms were bound close to her sides by chains of gold. On her head was a helmet. The streets and windows and housetops were crowded with spectators eager to see Aurelian and his great prize, the captured Queen of the East.

No one is certain what happened to Zenobia after this. Some historians believe she married a Roman senator and enjoyed a private life of wealth and ease at his estate near Rome, and the luxury of dying at home in bed. As for Aurelian, he was killed by a group of army officers in the year A.D. 275.

Zenobia

Eleanor of Aquitaine

1 1 2 2 - 1 2 0 4

E leanor of Aquitaine was one of the most vivid and extraordinary figures of the Middle Ages. As queen of France, queen of England, and mother of two kings, Richard and John, she exerted great influence on the course of human events in Europe. So different was her behavior from the inferior role ordained for her sex that men who could not tolerate such independence spread the story that she must be a demon.

A demon? No, she simply was one of those great women who leaped over the barriers of proper behavior set for her sex. She did as she pleased, no matter what others said. Great as her impact was on politics, she also shaped the literary and artistic life of her time, as well as the ideals and codes of chivalry. A modern-day historian calls her "the sex symbol of her age, for she was as beautiful as she was regal, and universally admired."

Eleanor was born in 1122. She was the daughter of William X, duke of Aquitaine and count of Poitiers. She was named after her mother, who not long

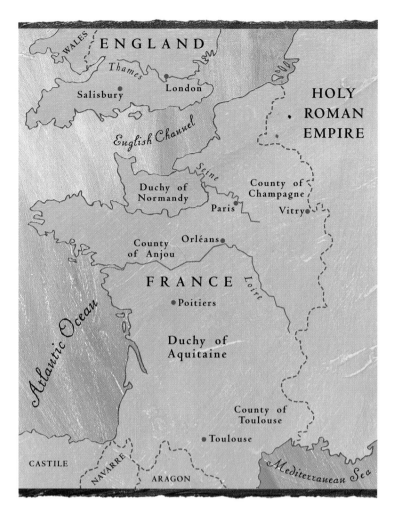

after bore two other children, a girl, Petronilla, and a boy, William, who was destined to be his father's heir.

William X ruled over one of the largest domains in France, larger in fact than that held by the king of France. In the twelfth century, France was the name of a geographical region rather than of a country. The region was divided among several peoples who spoke different languages. The king ruled little more than the neighborhood around Paris and Orléans. He was only the foremost among a great many noblemen. Although under feudal custom they were his vassals, these noblemen ruled larger regions than the king's. Eleanor's homeland, the duchy of Aquitaine, was the greatest of these regions, including almost the whole of southwest France from the river Loire to the Pyrenees.

Beyond the king's small area lay a patchwork of duchies and counties. In some of these regions, no central figure was in control. But others were dominated by strong magnates with as much or more power than the king. The king was obliged to play deadly games with dukes and barons to secure some sort of balance of power, however shaky.

The twelfth century was a great time for the making of myths. Many nobles invented family histories that gave them legendary ancestors. Often they did so to cover up plain origins. The common people enjoyed, and many probably believed, these fictions. Eleanor's son, King Richard the Lion-Hearted, laughed at his own family's pedigree. "We come from the Devil," he said, "and must needs go back to the Devil."

Eleanor's Aquitaine probably got its name from the great rivers and their tributaries that watered its fertile plains. Her ancestors were not only soldiers and administrators but patrons of scholars and philosophers. The family kept a treasury of books acquired by exchange with other rulers or on loan from the libraries of the monasteries. Her grandfather William IX was the first to write what would later be called troubadour poetry.

At birth, Eleanor had disappointed her parents. Why? Because she was not a boy, the male heir they so passionately desired. (They could not know how this daughter would outshine all the Williams before her, and would change history.) But Eleanor's parents soon realized what a sturdy, lively, talented child they had produced. She stood out among the many girls neighboring nobles had sent to the duchess for the customary training in the aristocratic way of life. Living in the ancestral palace at Poitiers, Eleanor was surrounded by retainers: chaplains and clerks and cooks and falconers and minstrels and scribes and dozens of humbler folk assigned to servants' tasks.

Unlike most of her contemporaries, male and especially female, Eleanor was well educated. That was uncommon, for it was then generally believed that women should be trained to spin and sew, embroider and sing, keep quiet, and not think for themselves. Eleanor had no interest in such activities. Early on she was taught to read and write and to do arithmetic. She studied Latin literature, of course, for Latin was the language of educated people everywhere.

Young Eleanor was exposed to a rich variety of ideas. Her father, William X, was very fond of his eldest daughter and made her his constant companion. With Eleanor at his side, he was always traveling about, administering justice and bringing rebellious vassals under control. Eleanor was in and out of abbeys and palaces and castles, observing the life around her and picking up the do's and don'ts of effective government. On these trips she learned a great deal about politics, about winning and holding power.

When Eleanor was only eight she lost both her mother and her brother. They died within a few months of each other. Deprived now of her mother's warmth and guidance, she also missed her father's companionship. For William, a notorious hothead, had become embroiled in conflicts with both counts and cardinals. Ultimately his high-handed actions so displeased the church that the pope excommunicated him.

In 1137, when Eleanor was fifteen, her father died. And Eleanor became the duchess of Aquitaine. If a man had no son, his daughter became the sole heir. Under feudal law women could inherit a domain, receive homage from its vassals, and lead them into war. They held land in their own right and fulfilled family obligations to fight and to rule just like men.

Whom would she marry? She and her immense domain were highly desirable. Feudal marriages were not for love, but for material advantage to both sides. Eleanor was speedily betrothed to the only surviving son of Louis VI, king of France.

This lad, to become Louis VII, was only sixteen. But marriage in the Middle Ages between children even younger than this was not uncommon. Louis had been steered toward the priesthood and had been educated as a "child monk" at the abbey of St. Denis, headed by the famous abbot Suger. It was not a training that equipped him to rule.

Just one month after the two young people married, Louis VI died, and his son inherited the throne of France. Now Eleanor was queen of France, as well as duchess of Aquitaine.

In feudal times, kings were considered to be divinely chosen and ordained, but personally responsible for the people. The king was the state; the community was supposed to carry out his wishes. While the king sat at the top of the pyramid of power by divine right, the same notion of paternal authority carried on down through the lesser powers. Duke, count, baron, the father of a family too—all administered justice to those subordinate to them. The king and these others were obliged to consult their chief vassals on matters of justice and policy.

The queen? She was due the same respect as the king. But unless she held power on her own, this was more a matter of personal courtesy.

Did kings and queens look the part? Well, not if you expected a great physical presence. Men and women in twelfth-century Europe were not tall. Five feet ten inches was considered a great height. The average man was about five feet two, and women were even shorter. Feminine beauty, judging by the literature, meant blond curly hair, gray eyes set wide apart, a straight nose, white skin, very red lips in the shape of a cupid's bow, a long neck and waist, slender, firm breasts, and long shapely fingers. We have no portraits of Eleanor, except for the effigy on her tomb, but the chronicles of her time tell us she was considered a great beauty.

If a man made it past childhood, he could expect to live into his thirties or forties. Women were at greater risk because of the hardships of childbirth. However, if a woman survived her childbearing period, she was more likely to live into old age than her husband. Eleanor, for example, bore ten children, lived an extremely active life, and died at eighty-two. Her two husbands died much before her, both of them from circulatory problems.

When Louis and Eleanor arrived in Paris in 1137 to rule over the kingdom, they at first made no great impression. Louis returned to his studies with the monks at Notre-Dame, fasting with them, keeping their vigils, singing in the choir. He dressed and behaved in such a simple fashion that no stranger would think him a king.

As for Queen Eleanor, she delighted in the schools that drew students, French and foreign, to hear the great teachers dispute matters of logic, philosophy, and religion. There was not yet a University of Paris, but schools had sprung up on the left bank of the Seine, the river that winds through Paris, where the students overflowed the lodgings and taverns. All kinds of instruction were offered: the liberal arts, civil and canon law, medicine, and theology. Master Peter Abelard was in Paris lecturing on what the angry bishops of the church called false doctrine. People should not look to authority for answers, Abelard said, but to reason, for reason as well as faith was a gift from God. He urged that no one teach what that person himself did not understand, and he taught that to challenge authority with questions was the way to discover truth as well as error. To the dismay of the church, the noble ladies of the court as well as students swarmed around Abelard to drink in his message. Eleanor must have enjoyed the learned debates that the king arranged in the palace gardens. She savored the new spirit of inquiry that would make France a center of humanism.

Paris, the "king's town," the political and religious capital, had some 200,000 people squeezed into its small area. At its heart was the Île-de-France, an almond-shaped island in the Seine dominated at either end by the walled citadels of the

*Eleanor
of Aquitaine*

47

Notre-Dame

king and the archbishop. The old basilica of Notre-Dame raised its white mass over a labyrinth of crooked streets. On the right bank was the business quarter, with its money changers, shops, markets, and boats crowding the river port. Churches large and small displayed mosaics or carvings depicting the epic of salvation. The upper stories of the tall houses of the burghers stuck out over the narrow streets. On either side of the Seine, suburbs had begun to encroach on the orchards and vineyards of the surrounding lands.

In those early years, Louis VII made a promising start as king. He had got off the mark with a marriage that tripled the size of his domains. Honest and direct, he felt he could handle his vassals and deal with anyone, at home or abroad, who threatened him. But as time passed, Eleanor saw him again and again erupt in a savage temper and display a lack of judgment that did great harm.

Soon after Louis took the throne he had to put down a rebellion in the town of Orléans. Its people complained bitterly about heavy taxation and demanded a charter of rights. Louis marched on the town and swiftly executed the leaders of the uprising. Then he abruptly decided to grant most of the reforms demanded. The reversal of his position, the inability to make up his mind, became all too typical in Eleanor's view.

Not long after, a rebellion broke out in Eleanor's domain, in her own capital city of Poitiers. The people did not want to see a foreign king take them over simply because their land was part of Louis's wife's domain. So they boldly declared Poitiers to be a free city. Louis marched his army on the town and captured it easily. Instead of just taking control, however, the enraged king ordered that all the children of its leading citizens be rounded up as hostages and sent into exile. Then, hearing the howls of the anguished parents, he abruptly changed his mind and let everyone go free.

Eleanor saw this as a weakness; it lessened her respect for him. Perhaps to test his courage, she decided that Louis ought to invade the county of Toulouse in southern France. It belonged to her, she said, because her grandmother had been the daughter of the count of Toulouse and she had been done out of her inheritance. Prodded by Eleanor, Louis saw that to capture Toulouse would not only enlarge his kingdom but enhance his own personal reputation. But Louis had no military sense, and when his poorly organized army met a strong defense, he turned tail and fled.

We can imagine Eleanor's feelings about this fiasco. Men were supposed to be brave and bold, ready to dare all for honor and glory. Did she make Louis think he had to be a killer before he could be loved or respected?

He soon got into serious trouble with the pope over the appointment of bishops, arrogantly taking over what was the church's responsibility. The pope promptly not only excommunicated him but also ordered that in any town or castle where Louis dwelled, no bells could ring, no church services be held, and no marriages, confessions, baptisms, or burials could take place. In a time when people worried deeply about their souls and clung to church rituals, this was terrible punishment for offenses not they, but their king, had committed.

Still another disaster occurred when Louis and Eleanor quarreled with Count Theobald of Champagne and the pope took Theobald's side. Determined to defy the pope and to humble Theobald, Louis, with Eleanor's support, personally led an army into Champagne and laid it waste. When he reached the town of Vitry, the people were stunned by the savage attack. The troops set their houses ablaze, and as the fire spread, the terrified citizens ran into their church, taking the sick, the elderly, and the children with them. The church was the traditional sanctuary where noncombatants could always find safety.

Watching from the hill above, Louis saw the flames race toward the church.

As it was engulfed in fire, the screams of the citizens trapped inside split the air. In a few minutes the timbers of the roof fell in, burying the charred bodies of 1,300 people. The whole town was destroyed.

Louis was riven by guilt, but he did not call off the war. In the winter of 1143–44, village after village fell to his bloodthirsty troops, now augmented by thieves and murderers who joined up to share in the loot. Suffering nightmares, the king—no longer a boy, but a haggard and depressed man—found little solace in Eleanor. Her husband had failed to be the powerful mate she had desired, and she herself had failed to provide the country with the male heir it expected. Had she too, like Louis, somehow offended God?

Seeking help, Eleanor turned to Saint Bernard, whose abbey of Clairvaux was in Champagne. Head of the Cistercian order, he had dominated western Christendom for many years. He said to her:

Seek, my child, those things that make for peace. Cease to stir up the king against the church and urge upon him a better course of action. If you will promise to do this, I in turn promise to entreat the merciful Lord to grant you offspring.

On Eleanor's urging, Louis made peace with the church. And in 1145, Eleanor gave birth, not to the boy the kingdom wanted, but to a daughter named Maria, who would one day become countess of Champagne. As for Louis, he never fully recovered from the crime of Vitry. To ease his guilt, he helped rebuild the burned town and wore a hair shirt next to his skin. He fasted and he prayed, but it was not enough. What ordeal should he undergo to wipe out his sin?

The answer was given him when a new pope, Eugenius III, decided late in 1145 to launch the Second Crusade. He called upon Louis and his vassals to march to the Holy Land to save it from the "infidel" (the Moslems). The fragile kingdom of Jerusalem, founded after the First Crusade, was under assault by the Turks. All who joined in the crusade, the pope promised, would receive forgiveness for their sins.

Louis's first appeal for support got only a lukewarm response from his vassals. The pope then asked Saint Bernard to preach a crusade. At Easter in 1146, the abbot made a passionate appeal to an immense crowd standing in the open fields. His fiery eloquence swept up not only the great nobles but simple folk as well, who deserted their villages and towns by the thousands to join in. Many joined not in the service of Christ but to get rich on plunder.

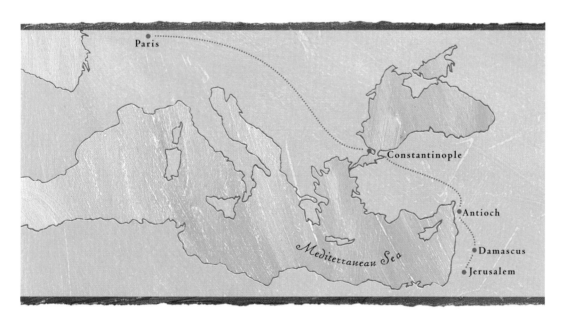

Eleanor too vowed to go. This was no precedent, for princesses had accompanied their husbands on the First Crusade fifty years earlier. Eleanor was joined by other great ladies—indeed, so many, with their retainers, that men grumbled at the burdens the women imposed.

Who would pay the enormous costs of a prolonged crusade? The people, of course. Landlord or peasant, noble or merchant, clergy or layman—all were heavily taxed under the threat of excommunication.

The 3,000-mile journey to Jerusalem was a difficult and dangerous pilgrimage. They left France in June of 1147 and reached Constantinople in October. Constantinople sits on a triangular site jutting out into the Bosporus, a strait that separates Europe from Asiatic Turkey. In Eleanor's time it was the richest city in the known world. The crusaders rested there for three weeks in the Greek emperor's palace, dazzled by its splendor: the gold throne, the pavements of precious marble, the glowing mosaic pictures, the exotic foods served at luxurious banquets.

Here the material civilization of ancient Greece and Rome had never ended. Eleanor marveled at the plumbing, the drainage, the central heating, the advanced medicine, and the finery of Eastern fashions. She would introduce all these on her return home.

But when the crusaders resumed their journey, discipline broke down as wintry storms and floods ruined the tents and baggage and killed men and horses. Then came attacks by Turkish bowmen on fast ponies, with many more crusaders killed. At one point they took ship in the hope of evading assaults, only to be lashed by terrific storms for three weeks.

Not until the spring of 1148 did they reach the Syrian city of Antioch, whose villas, palaces, and gardens were as dazzling as Constantinople's. Here Eleanor met her uncle, Raymond of Poitiers, who had become the ruler of Antioch by marrying its princess. Although older than Eleanor, he was a handsome, powerful, and gallant prince who made Louis seem all the more ineffectual and insignificant. When rumors reached Louis that Raymond and Eleanor were having an affair, the king was wildly jealous. This marked the beginning of the end of their marriage.

They quarreled, they threatened each other, there were long, icy silences. Finally Louis forced Eleanor to leave Antioch with him and go on to Jerusalem. As if to show his mettle, Louis joined a military expedition against the Moslem city of Damascus. It ended in still another bloody failure. The crusaders stayed in Jerusalem for another year, but lacking the power to entrench themselves and

suffering from internal dissension, they left at last for home, with Eleanor and Louis sailing in separate ships.

After Louis and Eleanor returned to France, the pope arranged a reconciliation, and a second daughter was born. But five years later, in 1152, their marriage was dissolved. According to feudal custom, Eleanor retained the duchy of Aquitaine.

Two months later, she married Henry Plantagenet, count of Anjou (a province of western France) and the grandson of Henry I of England. Henry was only eighteen, and Eleanor, twenty-nine. When young Henry succeeded to the throne as Henry II, in 1154, Eleanor went from having been queen of France to being queen of England. The result was that England, Normandy, and the west of France were united under Henry's rule. This made him the most formidable monarch in western Europe.

Henry neither looked nor acted like the youngster he was. A big man with boundless energy, he had a large head, a freckled face, blue-gray eyes, and red hair and beard. He had a will of iron and an ability to work that astonished everyone. Calm and warm most of the time, he could erupt in sudden rages, smashing furniture or striking out with fist or sword at anyone unlucky enough to be close by. He was an able military leader, but unlike his son Richard the Lion-Hearted he did not relish war for its own sake. He was generous to the poor, giving alms often. He had a scholarly side too, mastering several languages, reading widely, and enjoying discussions with intellectuals.

Henry faced a monumental task when he took the throne. England was in great disorder. Robber barons, using mercenaries, rode out of their castles to raid the countryside, robbing people of their goods and torturing or killing all who resisted. They burned down villages and destroyed crops, causing mass starvation. England was so miserable that men said "Christ and his saints slept."

Henry seized control at once. He built roads, bridges, and dikes; improved markets and fairs; repaired castles on the frontiers. He tore down the evil men's strongholds, kicked out the mercenaries, restored lands and manors to their rightful owners. He traveled the whole country, settling lawsuits, punishing criminals. He assigned judges to ride on circuit to meet local needs, restored order and honesty in the collection of taxes, encouraged the development of local juries. Peace and prosperity seemed at hand.

Eleanor traveled with Henry, riding on horseback or in wagons. She admired her husband's energy, his decisiveness, and his ability to analyze problems and settle them quickly. When Henry was absent, she helped dispense justice, settled disputes, and kept track of tax receipts. She proved to be a highly efficient sovereign.

To her new husband Eleanor bore eight children in thirteen years: five sons and three daughters. Perhaps she thought that if she married a younger man she could control him. She quickly learned how wrong she was. Though he had loved her for her beauty and her intelligence, that did not prevent him from having mistresses.

Not long after Eleanor had her last child, John, Henry's love affairs became too open and frequent for Eleanor to tolerate. Now, at forty-six, she was considered elderly. Bitter and lonely, she reminded herself that she was not only queen of England but sovereign of Aquitaine. She decided to take into her own hands the wealth and the freedom it offered. In 1169 she moved her household into the palace at Poitiers. She gave much attention to developing her sons' political skills, preparing them for the power they would one day exert.

Eleanor's feudal world was kept in an uproar by rude and barbarous barons whose ideal was troublemaking. Her hope was to end the disorder by molding the younger generation into civilized people who would know how to respect women and live peaceably.

She knew she was struggling against a powerful current, but she did her best to make up for past abuses suffered by the people. She journeyed to the far corners of her region, bringing together feuding vassals, trying to establish justice and order in a traditionally ungovernable province.

Eleanor believed not just in the equality of the sexes but in the superiority of women. Removing herself from the harsh authoritarian world of masculine kingship, she welcomed to her court dozens of noblewomen whose talents flourished under her encouragement.

Eleanor made her court a center of culture and the arts. The most famous poets and troubadours of the time enjoyed her patronage. The troubadour's art had flowered with Eleanor's grandfather, William IX. Troubadours were composers and performers of lyric poetry sung to the accompaniment of viol, rebec, or tabor. They traveled from castle to castle to entertain their patrons. Their poetry drew on Celtic folklore and legend, with its mythology, monsters, and magic. Chrétien de Troyes, at Eleanor's suggestion, wrote the first great literary treatment, in rhymed couplets, of the legend of King Arthur and the Knights of the Round Table. There were female poets too. At least twenty

troubadour

Eleanor
of Aquitaine

have been identified among the troubadours who flourished in Eleanor's time.

The subject of love commanded such a great interest in her court that one writer published a book about it, based partly on Eleanor's rules for the game of love. In one song an older woman instructs a maiden pleading the cause of a knight:

Maiden, if he really wants my love,
he'll have to show high spirits and behave,
be frank and humble, not pick fights with any man,
be courteous with everyone;
for I don't want a man who's proud and bitter,
who'll debase my worth or ruin me,
but one who's frank and noble, loving and discreet . . .

This peaceful interlude at her court came to an end in five years. Trouble began when Henry ordered Eleanor to turn over the province's tax revenues to his own treasury. She refused, and in 1173, with the support of three of her sons, she rose in revolt against her husband. Her aim apparently was to reduce Henry's power or depose him, and to regain the independence of Aquitaine.

Did the king suspect Eleanor was plotting against him? Perhaps not, for he did not appreciate that women too may desire power and fight for it. Henry and Eleanor's three eldest sons—Henry, now eighteen; Richard, sixteen; and John, fifteen—had come to detest their father for his refusal to give them any authority. Young though they were, in that time they were considered to be adults. Restless and ambitious, they wanted to be allowed some power, but Henry treated them like helpless dependents. Eleanor secured the military support of her first husband, Louis, who had his own grievances against Henry to settle.

Hiring thousands of mercenaries, Henry put down the revolt. In 1174 Eleanor was captured fleeing in men's clothes, astride a horse. She was brought back from France to England and kept in comfortable but strict confinement in a castle at Salisbury. Henry made peace with his sons, giving each enough, he thought, to appease them.

Eleanor's imprisonment ended only with the death in 1189 of Henry II. Free at last at the age of sixty-seven, she played a political role even greater than before. As her son Henry had died years before, Richard was crowned king. Eleanor wielded considerable power as her son's principal adviser. She arranged his marriage to Berengaria, daughter of the king of Navarre. She put down John's rebellion when Richard was away on crusade, and she ruled over England herself when Richard was imprisoned in Austria on his way back from the crusade. An immense ransom was demanded for his release. Eleanor personally oversaw the collection of the funds from many sources and went to Austria herself to obtain Richard's freedom and escort him home.

In 1199 Richard died of an arrow wound received during the siege of a castle. He left no heir to the throne, so his brother John was crowned king. Nearly eighty now, Eleanor tried loyally to support John, although she knew well how he alienated everyone by his deceit and treachery.

Finally Eleanor gave up on political life. She retired to the abbey of Fontevrault to spend her last days among its nuns. She died in 1204, at the age of eighty-two. She was buried in the abbey, next to her husband Henry and her son Richard.

Isabel of Spain

1 4 5 1 - 1 5 0 4

Where could you find, today or in the past, such a woman as Isabel, queen of Spain? She was "stronger than a strong man, more constant than any human soul, a marvelous example of honesty and virtue," said Peter Martyr, an Italian scholar at Isabel's court. "Nature has made no other woman like her."

A modern biographer of Isabel agrees: "Truly extraordinary," writes Peggy Liss, "is the extent to which her powerful intellect and powerful will interacted with her will to power in becoming the monarch she sought to be. Europe had no queen as great until the advent of England's Elizabeth I."

Decisions made by Isabel and her husband, King Ferdinand, changed the course of history. Under them, Spain was united into one kingdom. In 1492, after seven hundred years of occupation, the Moors were driven out of Granada, their last stronghold in Spain. The Moors were originally a nomadic people of North

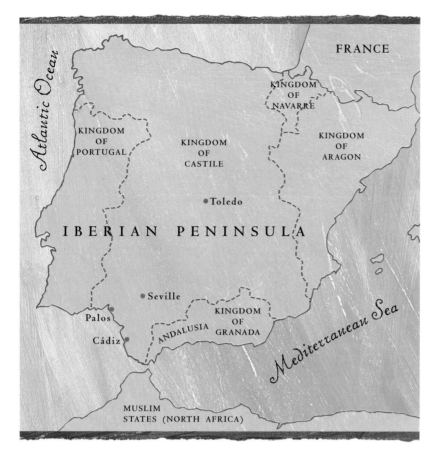

Africa. In the eighth century they were converted to Islam and became Muslims. Many spread northwest into Spain. In 1492, the Jews, who had lived in Spain for centuries, were expelled from their homeland. And Columbus was launched on his epochal voyages to America.

Linked to all this was the Spanish Inquisition. Guided by the monarchy, it was responsible for one of the longest and fiercest repressions in human history.

Isabel was born in 1451, the daughter of Juan II, the king of Castile, and his second wife, Isabel of Portugal. Ferdinand, the man she would marry, was born a year later, in 1452. He was the son of another Juan II, the king of Aragon. Both kingdoms—Castile and Aragon—were part of the Iberian peninsula. And so were three other kingdoms: Portugal, Navarre, and Granada. Within each of these five major kingdoms were several provinces, with their own histories, customs, and language dialects.

At birth Isabel was second in line for the crown of Castile, after her half brother Enrique, the king's child by his first wife. When Isabel was three, her father died, and Enrique, now thirty, succeeded to the throne. Isabel grew up without a father, and almost without a mother, for her mother went mad soon after her husband's death.

Franciscan monks had much to do with young Isabel's education. One of the priests who tutored her was a great admirer of Joan of Arc, who had been burned at the stake only twenty years before Isabel's birth. Isabel absorbed the story of the young French girl who heard the voices of saints urging her to take arms and lead men into battle to free her country from the English invaders. Later, when she was queen, Isabel would claim that as God alone had inspired Joan, so too had he inspired her actions.

Isabel mastered the usual domestic skills girls were taught. To be a spinner, a weaver, a mother—that was woman's destiny. No one expected that one day this child would rule Castile. The sons of kings and noblemen, on the other hand, were taught all there was to know about weapons and armor and horses. Prowess in war was the measure of a man's honor. Yet Isabel too became an accomplished rider and a fearless hunter.

Early on, Isabel came to believe that divine providence was directly active in human affairs. She was steeped in Roman Catholicism, with its holy days, its ceremony and ritual, its explanations of the universe and of human relationships as well. Her religion was militantly opposed to Islam, although all about her was the cultural and material presence of the Muslims, who had conquered much of Spain several hundred years before. Castile's churches, houses, towers, and walls were in the Moorish style. And everywhere were the Muslims themselves, and the

Moorish-style house

Jews too, both thought of as racially different, and therefore inferior. For in the Castile of Isabel's youth, Muslims and Jews did not live shut away from Christians, but alongside them. Many Muslims were skilled artisans and industrious farmers. The Moors made great contributions to art, architecture, medicine, and science. The Jewish minority were not only Castile's tax gatherers but the chief taxpayers. They were artisans, craftsmen, clerks, and poets too. When Jews converted to Christianity, they made excellent theologians, mystics, friars, and even bishops.

Isabel had not only a Spanish but a Portuguese heritage, on her mother's side. She knew how the Portuguese Prince Henry the Navigator was gaining renown by promoting the exploration of West Africa. Maybe one day his sailors would find a route to the Holy Land and reclaim it for the Christian faith. Isabel had heard rumors that somewhere beyond the Atlantic Ocean were both people to be Christianized and great wealth in gold to be harvested.

It was exciting to think she might one day lead the quest for unknown hidden lands, strange peoples, fabulous riches. For did she not come from great warriors, monarchs and saints, powerful men and women? Should not God, one day, let her know what part she was to play in making history?

A princess in her teens was inevitably a marriage pawn. What made Isabel even more desirable was the sudden death in 1468 of her younger brother, taken by the plague. This put seventeen-year-old Isabel next in line for the Castilian throne. Within a year she was married to Ferdinand, heir to the throne of Aragon. His kingdom was much smaller than hers and had only a tenth of the population of Castile. A year her junior, Ferdinand was sturdy, charming, and a fine athlete. Trained in the military arts, Ferdinand was also at home in Renaissance culture.

In Europe, this was the beginning of a golden age. Great artists, writers, and scholars lived and worked in that period. The roster of genius in western Europe is astounding. Think of the artists: Leonardo da Vinci, Michelangelo, Raphael, Botticelli, to name but a few in Italy; Hieronymus Bosch, Albrecht Dürer, Hans Memling, Hans Holbein in northern Europe. And in literature? Dante, Aretino, Rabelais, Erasmus, Sir Thomas More, Machiavelli.

Spain shared in the cultural awakening of the early Renaissance. Isabel herself learned Latin. Scholars began to be prized as much as warriors. Spanish noblemen entrusted their sons to the tutelage of Italian humanists. Yet all this activity was on the surface of a culture still medieval in many respects. Beneath, deep divisions existed.

When King Enrique, Isabel's elder half brother, died in 1474, she was proclaimed queen of Castile. At her coronation she wore an elegant gown glittering with jewels and a necklace set with gems and pearls. One observer noted her finely chiseled face and lively expression, and another called her "the handsomest lady I ever beheld." She was of medium height, fair and blond, her eyes a greenish blue, "her look gracious and honest."

In 1479, when his father died, Ferdinand took the throne of Aragon. Thus the two kingdoms, Castile and Aragon, came together in the persons of the "Catholic Kings," as they were called. Isabel and Ferdinand would have five children: four girls and a boy.

Spain was emerging as a country, but more by this personal connection than by formal political unification. (That would take considerable time.) Meanwhile, the two young people ruled jointly in both kingdoms, with each domain continuing its own system of government while cooperating through their monarchs.

Isabel and Ferdinand were organized and self-disciplined. They made daily lists of things that had to be done, and they kept personal notes on people and events that might one day be useful. They invited talented people to court and sought their opinions.

Isabel took the greater hand in the structuring of government and the administration of justice. Ferdinand concentrated on foreign affairs and military matters. When important decisions were to be made, they acted together, giving and taking advice in a generally harmonious way. They were hands-on monarchs. It was a remarkable partnership.

Both rulers believed they were responsible for the spiritual welfare of their subjects. What they ardently wished was to unite Castile and Aragon by religious uniformity. But several religions co-existed in Spain: Christianity, Islam, and

Judaism. How gain unity? The choice the Catholic monarchs made was to convert non-Catholics, or to expel them.

The principal instrument of that policy was the Inquisition. The Inquisition itself did not begin with the reign of Isabel. It dated back to the year 1208, when Pope Innocent III commanded members of the church to inquire into the beliefs and behavior of suspected heretics. Then in 1452 a papal bull had authorized the king of Portugal "to subdue pagans, and other unbelievers inimical to Christ, to reduce their persons to perpetual slavery and then to transfer forever their property to the Portuguese Crown."

What is heresy? The word comes from the Greek *hairesis*, meaning "choice." To make choices—in religion or anything else—would seem to be every person's right, so long as those choices do not harm anyone else. But those who hold to blind faith, to dogma, and believe their dogma to be a virtue, do not operate in a world of reason. They do not even pity those who lack their faith. No, they seek to force nonbelievers to convert to the one true faith, as they conceive it. To achieve that aim they submit the others to great mental and physical torture. And in the end, if the others do not convert, the true believers drive the others out of their world or kill them.

The Inquisition reached Spain when Isabel and Ferdinand asked Pope Sixtus IV to let them introduce it in Castile. He granted their request in 1478. The terror would last far beyond the monarchs themselves. During the next 350 years the Inquisition persecuted about 100,000 Jewish converts, known as *conversos*, for the heresy of Judaizing. The New Christians, as they were called, were charged with practicing Jewish rituals in secret. The great majority of the conversos saw all their property stripped away, to be divided between the Catholic majesties and the Holy Office—the two groups of officials conducting the Inquisition.

It began in Seville, a town reputed to be full of heretics. Isabel had two Dominicans, known for their hatred of conversos, appointed chief inquisitors for the region. She commanded the citizens to give them all the help they needed to ferret out heretics. The number of informers multiplied as frightened people turned in friends, neighbors, and even family members to assure their own safety. Thousands of conversos fled the city to seek shelter on the large estates of friendly nobles. But didn't the mere fact that they left mean they must be guilty? Suspicion, slander, and libel were often all the inquisitors needed to condemn anyone. The nobles who took in conversos were ordered to give them up or be arrested themselves.

The accused victims were isolated in prison cells and forced to confess in the presence of instruments of torture so gruesome that almost anyone would talk under the threat of such agonizing pain. Those who would not confess to heresy were turned over to the secular authorities to be burned alive. The executions were staged as public spectacles in the belief they would be religiously uplifting. One Dominican friar, Torquemada, made the chief inquisitor by Isabel, ordered at least 2,000 conversos to be burned at the stake. Thousands of others who died in prison were burned in effigy, while thousands more fled Spain. About 40,000 were "reconciled" to the church. That meant, if they repented, they gave up all their possessions and were sentenced to prison, often for life.

Why did Isabel and Ferdinand launch the Inquisition against the Jews? After all, Jews were not strangers. Some Jewish families had arrived from the Holy Land in the sixth century B.C., after the destruction of Solomon's Temple. But around the fourth century A.D., Jews in Spain began to suffer restrictions. Intermarriage was forbidden. Their liberties were curtailed, and both the Muslims and the Catholic kings allowed or encouraged various forms of persecution.

Still, Jewish culture flourished under the Catholic monarchies between the

Inquisition

eleventh and thirteenth centuries. Jewish physicians, diplomats, and financiers earned great standing and influence in court. (Isabel herself had many conversos in her service.) And under Muslim rule in Andalusia, Jewish poets and philosophers were highly esteemed between the tenth and twelfth centuries. The Iberian peninsula was the principal bridge between the Muslim and Christian cultures of the Middle Ages. Schools were founded in Toledo where Arab, Jewish, and Christian scholars collaborated in many works that opened a new era in medieval science.

In the fourteenth and fifteenth centuries, however, came calamities demonstrating that religious persecution in Spain had developed into racist persecution. Now Jews were being defined as a race, a strange people, a foreign people, a hostile people. And the very fact that conversos were especially prominent in medicine, in law, in banking, in government—even in the Church itself—made them highly suspect. No matter how they talked, looked, or behaved, no matter what contributions they made to Spanish culture, Jews they were and Jews they would remain: enemies in disguise.

By the time Isabel came to the throne of Castile, the resentment and the hatred that large masses of the Spanish people felt against Jews had been heated to a fever pitch. No one could forget the pogrom in Seville, instigated by a Jew-hating priest, in 1341. Thousands of Jewish men were butchered in the streets, their wives and children sold into slavery.

Under such tremendous pressure, about 20,000 of the survivors converted to Christianity in the next decades. Then, in 1449, Toledo witnessed a bloody uprising against the Jews; it came to an end only when all conversos were removed from office and expelled from the city.

Isabel and Ferdinand saw hatred and violence spreading throughout their dominions. Unless the violence was stopped, it could destroy their rule. How could they avert disaster? One possible course would be to act at once to punish lawbreakers and the inciters of riots. This would end the chaos and win the support of citizens who disliked the constant turmoil and yearned for peace and stability.

On the other hand, the anti-converso forces, the racist demagogues, had become so strong that to contain the violent movement might require more military power than the monarchs could muster. What if three or four cities revolted at once? And would the use of repressive means cost them their popularity?

The method Isabel and Ferdinand chose was to establish the Inquisition. They told themselves it was the only way to prevent a bloodbath. They would not condemn Jews and conversos as a group, they would just punish individuals—the "guilty ones." The task of the Inquisition would be to investigate the validity of accusations made against individual suspects and then to pronounce sentence— guilty or innocent. That kind of Inquisition, controlled by the church, had long been operating in several Western countries. Why not in Castile?

Were the conversos actually practicing Judaism in secret, as the church charged? No, according to modern research. The great majority of New Christians had been assimilated by the time the Inquisition was launched. They had been integrated into the host culture to a very great degree. By persecuting Jewish converts, the Inquisition was foreshadowing the racist doctrine Adolf Hitler adopted when he launched the Holocaust. In Spain, too, the Jews were labeled a "race" inferior to pure-blooded Christians. For over two hundred years following the reign of Isabel and Ferdinand, Spaniards seeking office in the military or religious orders had to prove they were of pure Old Christian descent. How different was this from the race laws of Nazi Germany?

The next step in "purifying" and unifying Spain was to get rid of the Muslims. The only Muslim state surviving in Europe was the ancient and highly civilized kingdom of Granada in the southern part of Spain. In 1482, Isabel and Ferdinand launched a campaign to conquer it. About the size of Switzerland, the region had fourteen cities, a hundred fortified towns, and about 300,000 people, many of them refugees from the Inquisition.

Because Granada was torn by internal conflicts, the time was ripe for invasion. From the start this was called "Isabel's war." She took a direct interest in the conduct of the war and was responsible for improved methods of supplying her troops. Daily she sent in money and munitions, relentlessly demanding of everyone more men, more munitions, more mules. Hundreds of men served as her personal envoys (or spies) to see that her orders were carried out. Often she had to deal with rambunctious young knights who joined up in the hope of getting rich on booty, rather than to serve God. They had no place in the new kind of army she shaped, an army in which discipline, efficiency, and economy were made to count. Within decades, the Spanish army would evolve into the most powerful in Europe.

Having seen in earlier wars great suffering and needless deaths for lack of prompt medical aid, Isabel established a Queen's Hospital, to travel with the troops. For it she requisitioned medicines, bandages, slings, tents, and physicians. It was the first military hospital to move onto the battlegrounds of western Europe. Her medical units reduced war casualties so much that the innovation was copied by the military in other countries.

The one thing Isabel regretted was that as a woman she could not lead the troops into battle herself. But finally, after ten long years of war, Granada surrendered. That victory added a rich and important region to the territorial unification of Spain. Isabel, at forty, had achieved power and prestige unheard of for a female monarch.

Now she began the task of transforming the Muslim kingdom into a province of Catholic Spain. But, advised by such uncompromising churchmen as Torquemada, Isabel would not allow the Moors of Granada to settle down peaceably as Muslim vassals of Christian overlords. Her religious zeal dictated not only conquest but conversion. When initial efforts at preaching and persuasion accomplished little, Isabel turned to sterner measures: systematic persecution and forced baptism. (Later, in 1501, the Muslims were ordered to convert to Christianity or leave the country.)

With the country at peace, and Muslims no longer a threat, Isabel could focus on eliminating corruption throughout society. Behavior among the clergy considered highly immoral—such as homosexuality and the keeping of concubines—was punished savagely. She left no room for cultural or religious diversity.

As for the Jews, now that their numbers and wealth had shrunk, their value to Isabel diminished. And recent anti-Jewish riots were signs that public hatred was still mounting. So in 1492, Isabel decided that this remnant of a once highly esteemed people should be expelled. Deportation—the uprooting of a people from its native soil—was her solution.

On March 31, 1492, Isabel and Ferdinand ordered that all Jews refusing baptism must leave by July 1. All their property must be sold by that time, nor could they take any gold or silver with them. They would lose everything they had—home, land, business, profession, community—and be forced to seek new homes in strange lands.

A tiny minority agreed to baptism. The rest (estimates range from 75,000 to 200,000) clung stubbornly to their faith. Rather than give it up, the Jews left Spain in search of a better life.

In western Europe the forced exodus came as startling news. Only a few countries, however, voiced sympathy. How can Spain do this for the glory of religion? asked a Genoese; "the Jews are not beasts, but men created by God." England and France refused to accept Jews. But Portugal, Italy, Greece, Turkey, and North Africa let them in.

The monarchs postponed the date of departure from July 1 to August 2. This was the day before the Italian navigator, Christopher Columbus, set out with his fleet of three Spanish ships to chart a new route west to the riches of the Orient. He sailed from Palos, a small port, because the principal Spanish port, Cádiz, was tied up by other business of Their Majesties. Thousands of Jews were penned up in the holds of many ships departing from Cádiz.

The mission of Columbus, apart from the hunt for gold, was to extend the Catholic domain by converting the heathen of Asia to "our Holy Faith." After seven years of effort the Genoese sailor had finally convinced Isabel and Ferdinand to support his enterprise. After their victory over the Moors, the monarchs were ready to extend their power overseas. The Portuguese had already opened up a trade route to India and the Far East. Now, in 1492, it was more than time for Spain to move.

Although Isabel had long resisted Columbus's many overtures, she changed

her mind when he won the support of a powerful figure in her court, Luis de San-tangel. The manager of many of her financial responsibilities (and a converso), Santangel talked the queen into backing Columbus by offering to find at least half the necessary money. Columbus would come up with the other half, probably borrowed from Italian investors. With money no longer a troublesome issue, Isabel could not resist so dramatic and daring a project. Reluctantly, because the queen insisted, Ferdinand went along with her decision. We're taking so small a risk, she argued, for so large a possibility of glory to God and church, and of profit to our kingdoms and treasury.

Columbus never reached the Orient. Instead, when he landed on the shores of the islands that we now call the West Indies, he "discovered" what already existed but had remained unknown to him and to the people of Europe. His undertaking radically changed the way the world looked at itself. His voyages inaugurated a profound change in human history—ushering in a new era of slavery and colonialism, whose ravages still burden the earth.

The backing Isabel gave Columbus was inspired by the hope of great wealth. By the time he died, in 1504, the dream of great riches had begun to fade. It revived in 1519 and later, when the Spanish conquistadors Hernán Cortes and Francisco Pizarro shattered the Aztec and Inca empires of Mexico and Peru

and opened their treasures and resources to Spanish exploitation. Spanish control quickly extended from the original Caribbean bases founded by Columbus all through South America and then up into the southern and southwestern regions of North America.

The last decade of Isabel's reign brought her great grief due to the deaths of her only son, Juan, her daughter Isabel, and her grandson Miguel. Isabel left no diary or memoirs. But in her will she spoke of what mattered most to her: the unity of Spain, the reform of the church, the codification of the laws of Castile. She regretted the abuses suffered by the Native Americans, and especially their enslavement by Columbus and others, which she now opposed. For the "red men," she said, have souls.

As she lay dying, she begged the family and courtiers around her bedside not to weep for her, but to pray for her soul. She died on November 26, 1504, at the age of fifty-five. When Ferdinand died in 1516, he was buried beside Isabel in the Franciscan monastery at Granada.

Elizabeth I

1 5 3 3 - 1 6 0 3

Good Queen Bess" her people called her. But "good" is a tame word for one of the most remarkable women who ever lived. Elizabeth I came to the throne of England in 1558 at the age of twenty-five. It was not a happy time for a young woman to take the responsibility for ruling a kingdom. Religious conflicts, a huge government debt, and heavy losses in a war with France had brought England low. But by the time of Elizabeth's death forty-five years later, England had experienced one of the greatest periods in its long history. Under Elizabeth's leadership, England had become united as a nation; its industry and commerce, its arts and sciences had flourished; and it was ranked among the great powers of Europe.

Elizabeth was the daughter of King Henry VIII and his second wife, Anne Boleyn. At the age of two she lost her mother when Henry had Anne's head chopped off. Not a good start for a child. But her father placed her in the care of one lord or lady after another, and the lively little girl with the reddish-gold hair, pale skin, and golden-brown eyes won everyone's affection.

Almost from her infancy Elizabeth was trained to stand in for ruling men, in case the need should arise. So she had to master whatever they were expected to know and do. Her tutors found the child to be an eager student. She learned history, geography, mathematics, and the elements of astronomy and architecture. She mastered four modern languages—French, Italian, Spanish, and Flemish—as well as classic Greek and Latin. She wrote in a beautiful script that was like a work of art. The earliest portrait painted of her—when she was thirteen—shows a girl with innocent eyes holding a book in her long and delicate hands, already confident and queenly in her bearing.

She was a strong-willed girl who liked to give orders. She loved to be out on horseback, and rode so fast it frightened the men assigned to protect her. She loved dancing too—she never gave it up. Even in her old age she was seen one moonlit night dancing by herself in the garden.

Elizabeth had a half sister, Mary, born of Henry's first wife, Catherine of Aragon. Many years later came Elizabeth, the child of Anne Boleyn, and four years after, her half brother, Edward, the son of Henry's third wife, Jane Seymour. After Henry died, because succession came first through the male, ten-year-old Edward was crowned king. But he lived only another six years. Now Mary took the throne and, soon after, married King Philip II of Spain, a Catholic monarch like herself. He was twenty-seven and she thirty-eight. But they were rarely together, each ruling their own kingdom. Mary died of cancer at the age of forty-two. That made Elizabeth the monarch.

When she came to the throne on November 17, 1558, it was a day to be marked by celebrations, then and long after. As Her Majesty passed down a London street, an astonished housewife exclaimed, "Oh, Lord! The Queen is a woman!" For there were still many who could scarcely believe they were to be ruled by another woman. Elizabeth herself would say with mock modesty that she was "a mere woman." But everyone soon learned she was a very special woman. "Am I not a queen because God has chosen me to be a queen?" she demanded.

As princess and later as queen, Elizabeth lived in various palaces, with much coming and going; each time she moved, she took along her household staff of 120 people. Often the changes were required because there was no sanitation. The smelly palaces had to be emptied so they could be "aired and sweetened."

Even before Elizabeth came of age there was much talk of when she would marry, and whom. Marriages among the nobility and royalty were arranged not for love, but for practical reasons—to add land holdings, to strengthen the prestige and power of families, to cement an alliance of nations against a common enemy.

And remember, from the most ancient times, kings claimed that they as men were born to rule by divine right. That is, God had ordained that the crown should pass through the male line of descent. But when the king's wife had no male child, it meant trouble. Who then would rule? That crisis often led to civil war as various factions battled for the power to name a king. Many disputed Elizabeth's right to the throne, and as long as she had neither husband nor successor, her life was in danger.

Ever since Elizabeth was eight, however, she had said again and again, "I will never marry." Did marriage look promising to a girl whose father had had six wives, two of whom, including her own mother, he had beheaded? Yet she liked to hear of people who wanted to marry her.

And there was no shortage of suitors. She continued to insist she wished to live unmarried. No matter how often she said it, men did not believe it. Understandably, since she often made a prince or duke who had come to court her believe she was finally ready to give in—only at the last moment to back out. Once,

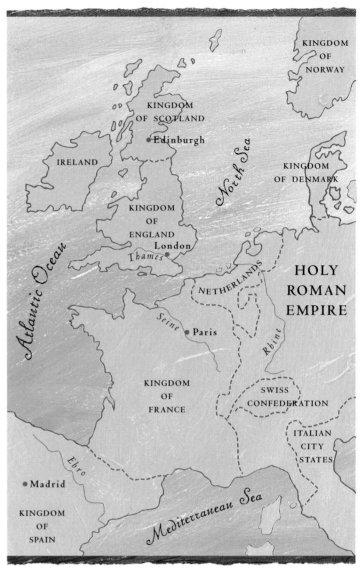

Elizabeth I

to a delegation from Parliament come to beg her to marry, she declared, "I am already bound unto a husband, which is the Kingdom of England."

And why should she, the absolute ruler of England, allow a man to sit alongside her as king? The power of husbands over wives in that century—and even now, in many places of this world—was so great that a husband might snatch the reins of power from her and leave her with the title but not the authority she loved to exercise.

Was it fun to be queen? As monarch, she commanded great wealth, inherited from her father, and people who wanted favors were always enriching her with lavish presents. She was no spendthrift, however. She hated to see money wasted, whether her own or the kingdom's. Early on she began keeping careful household account books, and later she would do the same with the royal accounts. Always she urged her counselors to carry out orders as inexpensively as possible.

Above everything else, Elizabeth wanted to have her people think well of her. Her deepest desire was to assure them of peace and prosperity. And why not make a grand personal impression upon them at the same time? In her mature years she gave free rein to her love of jewels and staged brilliant displays for the court and the people. Her dresses were decorated with large rubies, emeralds, and diamonds, and she wore jeweled necklaces, bracelets, and rings. In her hair, at her ears, and around her neck she wore pearls—the symbol of virginity.

During her reign she made many great processions through London, the people wild with excitement, crowding the streets—for the English, like most people, loved spectacle. In the first of them, her coronation, she wore gold robes as she was crowned. Trumpets sounded, pipes and drums played, the organ pealed, bells rang. Then came the state banquet in Westminster Hall. It began at 3:00 P.M., and went on till 1:00 A.M.

Elizabeth was often entertained at house parties. One of them, given by the Earl of Leicester in Kenilworth Castle, lasted for eighteen days in July. Thirty other distinguished guests were invited. The great number of their servants (together with Leicester's) turned the palace into a small town. When darkness fell, candles glittered everywhere, indoors and out, creating a fairyland. Musicians

sang and played, the guests danced in the garden, and such a great display of fire-works exploded that the heavens thundered and the castle shook. Then came a pleasure relished in those days: the hideous sport of bear-baiting. A pack of dogs was let loose in an inner courtyard to scratch and bite and tear at thirteen tormented bears. Still, the happy guests retained their appetite for a "most delicious banquet of 300 dishes."

The tremendous festival at Kenilworth was only one of the highlights of Elizabeth's summer festival. She moved from one great house to another all season long, always at the enormous expense of her hosts. They had little to complain of, however, for their wealth was often the product of the queen's generous bestowal of special privileges. In recognition of his high rank and in return for his support, she granted the Duke of Norfolk a license to import carpets from Turkey free of duty. The Earl of Essex was favored with the profitable right to tax imported sweet wines. Other pets got rich from a monopoly on the importation of or taxation of silks, satins, salt, tobacco, starch.

England was a small nation at that time: less than four million people, about as many as live in Arizona today. But the English were a young people, coming to maturity with new worlds opening up to them, in the mind and across the seas. A rebirth of culture—the Renaissance—had begun in the 1400s. With the revival of interest in the literature of the ancient Greek and Roman worlds came the beginning of a great age of discovery. This period marked the transition from medieval to modern times. The arts and sciences were influenced by changes in economic life. All the nation was swept up in the vast tides of change. Merchants, bankers, the gentry, artisans, seamen, miners—men and women of every class and condition—felt themselves part of the national venture.

At the heart of change in England was the queen. But no king or queen rules alone, no matter how authoritative or arrogant they may be. They usually look to others for advice, advice they may follow or reject. Elizabeth appointed ministers to handle the various departments of government, and made Sir William Cecil,

Shakespeare

then thirty-eight, her principal adviser. He was a brilliant, hardworking master of statecraft, devoted to her and England's well-being, and as ruthless as she and the nation's interests required. When he died in old age, his son Robert replaced him at her side.

So great was the queen's role, however, that her time became known as the Age of Elizabeth. Not only did many fine musicians flower, but writers too, such as Christopher Marlowe and John Donne and Ben Jonson and Edmund Spenser. And above all, the incomparable William Shakespeare, whose plays were sometimes performed at court. Astronomers, naturalists, mathematicians, geographers, and architects pioneered in their fields.

Then, too, there were the daring explorers who pushed English expansion overseas. One of the queen's favorites, Sir Walter Raleigh, planned the colony of Virginia in America and named it for her, the Virgin Queen. The queen herself put money into several of the great voyages, keeping close watch over the plans and their results. She supported Sir Francis Drake on his three-year voyage around the world, profiting mightily from the immense loot he captured from Spanish ships taken in the Pacific.

For Elizabeth, one of the most urgent problems was the question of religion. Her father had broken with the Catholic church and launched the English Reformation, creating the Church of England, with himself at its head. When Elizabeth's older half sister, Mary (who remained Catholic), married the Catholic king of Spain, Philip II, she reconciled England with the Church of Rome. In Mary's brief reign she persecuted those Protestants who refused to conform, executing some 270 of them.

When Elizabeth became queen upon Mary's death, she said she hoped religion would not prevent her people from living together in peaceful unity. She did not want to pry into people's souls or question their faith. But in 1570, Pope Pius V excommunicated her, denied her right to the throne, and declared her subjects owed her no allegiance. A directive from the pope's office decreed that the assassination of Queen Elizabeth would not be regarded as a sin. The effect of this directive was to turn practicing Catholics—about half of the English, most of them loyal—into potential traitors.

Though Elizabeth had wanted to pursue a middle way of toleration, circumstances threatened to overwhelm her. She had to beware of several Catholic monarchs of Europe who wished to see a Protestant England overthrown. Philip II of Spain sent ambassadors to England to urge Catholics to rise against Elizabeth, put her cousin Mary on the throne, and restore Roman Catholicism as the national faith. The line between power, politics, and religion was becoming very thin.

Missionary priests living abroad were sent into England to stir up opposition to the queen. But the English Catholics as a body never rebelled, nor did they ever intend to. Still, missionary priests such as Edmund Campion were convicted of plotting against Elizabeth and executed.

In 1588 a long-threatened invasion of England by Spain was launched by Philip II. He mistakenly believed that the English Catholics were waiting to welcome him. News of his armada of 130 big ships carrying 17,000 soldiers was terrifying. But the queen did not panic. She supervised the high command personally, meanwhile rallying popular support for the defense of the realm and sending troops to protect the coasts while Sir Francis Drake's ships set out to attack the Spanish fleet.

The Spanish Armada was defeated in three battles, its ships dispersed. When the news came of the tremendous victory, the citizens took to the streets, shouting for joy.

The defeat of the Spanish Armada did not end Spain's aggression against England. The Jesuits in England, who were especially identified with Spain, continued to be persecuted. Richard Topcliffe, a notorious hater of Catholics, was given authority to track down suspects. He examined them under torture to force information about people who had sheltered them. The treatment of them was so vicious and cruel that the victims welcomed death as a release from their agony.

During Elizabeth's reign several plots to assassinate her were uncovered. Elizabeth managed to give the impression that she was not frightened, but those close to her knew she was. When one of the major plots proved to center around Elizabeth's cousin, Mary Queen of Scots, Elizabeth found it almost intolerable to put to death a crowned queen. Yet she ordered the use of torture on Mary's co-conspirators, and in the end, Mary was beheaded. A song composed by William Byrd at the time suggests how ominous the news of a monarch's execution was:

> *The noble famous Queen*
> *Who lost her head of late*
> *Doth show that kings as well as clowns*
> *Are bound to fortune's fate,*
> *And that no earthly Prince*
> *Can so secure his crown*
> *But Fortune with her whirling wheel*
> *Hath power to pull them down.*

When two earls combined forces against her, Elizabeth's troops overcame them. The queen was so enraged she ordered that 800 of the mostly poor rebels be hanged. But she spared the lives of their wealthy leaders so that they might enrich her, either by buying their pardons or by forfeiting their lands.

*E*lizabeth the Queen always had a sharp eye out for profits. Her "sea dogs"—daring men like Sir Francis Drake and his cousin John Hawkins—led the way in challenging Spain's claim to the riches of the New World. Alas, the queen did not mind if their voyages included slave trading. In 1562 Hawkins sailed to the African coast of Guinea and loaded his three ships with 300 black slaves. Crossing the Atlantic, he sold the slaves at a great profit to planters on the island of Hispaniola (now Cuba).

The venture in slave trading proved so profitable that Elizabeth assigned her warship *Jesus of Lubeck* as flagship of Hawkins's squadron, and herself invested in Hawkins's next slaving voyage. His squadron made a series of raids on the African coast, rounding up 400 men, women, and children. He then sailed to South America, where he sold his human cargo. The rate of profit on this expedition—60 percent—must have been highly pleasing to Her Majesty.

Elizabeth came down hard on writers who criticized her actions. John Stubbs, a zealous Puritan, wrote a pamphlet expressing horror at the possibility the queen might marry a French Catholic. The queen had Stubbs and his publisher tried and convicted for seditious libel. How dare Stubbs say publicly she was too old to marry, and that the much younger French suitor could not possibly be in love with her? Elizabeth was merciless as she invoked the penalty for libel. With a butcher's cleaver, the executioner cut the right hands off Stubbs and his publisher. Not an uncommon punishment.

How did Elizabeth learn of all these plots and conspiracies? How did she know what plans Philip II of Spain was devising to invade her kingdom? Spies and secret agents—they were her eyes and ears. Crucial to the flow of information was Sir Francis Walsingham. Trained as a lawyer, he lived on the Continent for years, mastering the languages and the ins and outs of European affairs. Upon his return home, he was asked by Sir William Cecil, the queen's right arm, to gather information on the doings and plans of foreign governments. Soon he was made chief of England's secret service. He placed over seventy agents and

Elizabeth I

spies in the courts of Europe. And of course he watched closely the activities of people at home suspected of disloyalty. Letters to and from them were secretly opened, to nip plots in the bud.

Monarchs had absolute power. Elizabeth could arrest anyone, including the topmost ranks of the nobility, and imprison them in the Tower of London even if they had not committed any legal offense. The only thing that held her back was her fear of public opinion. It upset her when a crowd gathered at a public execution and was so disgusted by the butchery that they let out roars of disapproval. Still, like all rulers, Elizabeth said she believed that "born a sovereign princess," she enjoyed "the privilege common to all kings" and was "exempt from human jurisdiction and subject only to the judgement of God."

Despite her blazing nervous energy, Elizabeth was often sick. Her ailments were anxiously reported and discussed. For the English believed her survival was their only guarantee of freedom from foreign invasion and civil war. Once, suffering a raging toothache for the first time, the queen feared the pain of having an extraction. She had never had a tooth pulled and was terrified. To reassure her, an old friend, the Bishop of London, had her watch while the dental surgeon pulled out one of the bishop's own good teeth. And then she consented to have her own taken out.

It was commonly believed then that kings and queens had the magical power to cure disease in their subjects. Eager to demonstrate that she too had the sacred power of royalty, Elizabeth prayed intensely before using the royal touch on

people with scrofula, a nasty skin disease. Her chaplain said he watched "her exquisite hands, boldly, and without disgust, pressing the sores and ulcers." In one day it was reported that she healed thirty-eight persons. But if she did not feel divinely inspired, she would not try her touch.

Even in the last decade of her life, Elizabeth's energy was astonishing. She was as watchful as always over the affairs of state, though sometimes forgetful. But age made her more irritable; she sometimes shouted at her ladies and even boxed their ears. She was less able to control rival factions out for power, and became so fearful of assassins she rarely left her palaces.

A portrait of her done when she was approaching sixty shows her in a great white silk dress studded with aglets of black onyx, coral, and pearl. She wears three ropes of translucent pearls and stands on a map of England, *her* England. An ambassador reported that at sixty-three she looked old, but her figure was still beautiful, and her conversation was as brilliant and charming as ever.

There was dancing at court every evening, a pastime she still enjoyed. When it came to displays of gallantry by eager young men, she could act a bit vain and foolish, although never letting any hopeful get out of bounds.

In early 1603 Elizabeth developed a bad cold that led to a serious fever, and then she fell into a stupor for four days. As she lay dying, all of London became strangely silent. On March 24, the life of a rare genius ended. The nation went into mourning.

"Old age came upon me as a surprise, like a frost," she once wrote.

Elizabeth I

Christina of Sweden

1 6 2 6 - 1 6 8 9

Of all the queens in history, Christina of Sweden is one of the most discussed. Was she, as often charged, "shameless," "faithless," or "scandalous"? Or was that only gossip and rumor?

Christina inherited her throne at the age of six. She was the daughter of King Gustavus II Adolphus and Maria Eleanora of Brandenburg, a German principality. Her father, a great military hero, was a genius at creating new weapons and new ways to deploy troops. He modernized the organization of armies and built Sweden's forces into the first truly professional standing army in Europe.

War was on everyone's mind in the seventeenth century, the era of the Thirty Years' War (1618–48). This war began as a religious conflict between Roman Catholics and Protestants in Germany and broadened into a political struggle, with the Catholic Hapsburg dynasty trying to gain control of as much as possible of the Europe not yet within their empire. The powers on the other side, mostly Protestant, fought to hold the Hapsburg armies off. The configuration

of powers changed from time to time, as much of Europe was devastated, with great loss of life among civilians.

Protestant Sweden, led by King Gustavus, was involved in the great struggle. A huge man with tawny hair and beard, he was known as the Lion of the North. He had come to the throne of Sweden in 1611. Sweden was then somewhat larger than today's California, but half empty of human population, with a few towns lost in a mighty wasteland. (Today its population is still only 9 million, about the same as Michigan's.) Its chief products were iron, copper, and timber.

Gustavus was spectacularly successful in reorganizing the machinery of government, winning the support of the townspeople and the nobles. His knowledge of some ten languages and his remarkable gifts as a soldier had been developed in wars with Denmark, Russia, and Poland. His conquest of many lands, including Finland and Estonia, had made Sweden a powerful Baltic state.

Gustavus Adolphus was killed in 1632 while leading his troops into battle. His only child, Christina, became queen-elect. By orders her father left, she was educated as a prince. If this girl was to rule Sweden she must learn everything that men would be expected to learn. For the immediate future, power was exercised by her regent, Count Axel Oxenstierna, who had been the king's chancellor for a long time, handling affairs at home while Gustavus was off at the wars. The count had Christina taken away from her mentally ill mother.

In Axel Oxenstierna, the most important statesman of his time, the young queen had a rare treasure. She enjoyed his stories of heroes and villains, of wars won and lost, of diplomats and duchesses, of lovers and losers. His knowledge of the tides of history and his understanding of how decisions are made and mistakes learned from were of immense value to this fledgling ruler. "I loved this great man as a second father," she said later. "Although I knew almost all the greatest and most brilliant personalities of this time, I met few who could stand comparison with him."

Axel assigned a learned theologian, Johannes Matthiae, to tutor the child. He was a broad-minded man who gave the girl a solid grounding in history, the sciences, philosophy, and theology. He nourished her early passion for learning, her desire to understand the world around her and how monarchs ruled. She became skilled in several languages—Latin, Spanish, Italian, French, German. And she loved to write—letters, a journal, an autobiography.

On her eighteenth birthday, in 1644, Christina became queen in her own right. Early on, her ambition was to make her name famous for extraordinary merit rather than for military conquest. Honor and virtue were the qualities she admired most. Diplomats who attended the Swedish court noted that she shunned foolish talk and frivolous pleasures. They saw courage and strength of will in Christina. She was a born politician, they said, and had been trained to be among the best.

Christina and tutor

Christina came to think of herself as a heroine. She read avidly the biographies of great men of ancient times—such as Julius Caesar and Alexander the Great. And of course she knew well the achievements of her celebrated father. When she was still quite young and unable to distinguish between servile flattery and honest compliments, she thought everyone admired her. Later, however, she would realize how vain and proud she had been and would see this as the gravest of her faults. But in an era where absolute monarchs felt themselves to be chosen by God to rule over kingdoms, this egotism in a youngster is understandable. Was

she not the leader of the strongest military power in Europe? And had she not become an expert in the politics of government? It was easy to believe the homage she received was fully justified.

As studious and hardworking as she was, Christina found time for hunting, games, and sport. Her energy was astonishing. When out hunting she could stay in the saddle for ten hours at a stretch. Neither heat nor cold bothered her. She led the men and women of her court a hard life. Always on the go, she gave them no rest. When her ladies-in-waiting complained of the fast pace she set, she laughed and said, "If you are sleepy, go to bed. I can take care of myself." She usually slept fewer than five hours a night. She made no fuss over clothing or adornment and took less than fifteen minutes to dress. In her hair she wore only a single comb and a ribbon. Rarely, even in the worst weather, did she put on a hat.

As the years passed, people began to observe that she appeared rather unfeminine. She "looks more like a cavalry officer than a woman" was a typical remark. Few men felt attracted to such a figure. Someone who met Christina when she was about twenty-eight wrote: "She is of medium height, with high shoulders; her eyes are bright, and her nose is a little on one side. She has nothing feminine about her; even her voice is altogether masculine."

Several others made similar comments. No one described her as feminine.

When she was only seventeen she told Oxenstierna that she had no intention of ever marrying. And she never did. The gossipmongers could never accept that she was chaste or that she was dedicated to chastity. All sorts of rumors were spread—verbally and in print—about supposed secret love affairs, sensationalized to the point where it was claimed she had ordered the execution of a lover when she got tired of him. But there is no evidence that she ever did have a lover.

After Christina took the throne at age eighteen, conflict rose between herself and Oxenstierna. They differed over the conduct of the Thirty Years' War, which continued throughout the first four years of her reign. Although he opposed ending the war at that point, she was a prime mover in concluding the historic Peace of Westphalia. As soon as the war ended, class rivalries erupted in Sweden. An astute politician, Christina was able to keep the country from sliding into a bloody civil war. Yet she was unable to solve the tremendous economic problems that had been caused by the almost endless fighting.

The queen liked having intellectuals around her, and invited foreign scholars, musicians, and writers to her court. René Descartes (1596–1650), the eminent

In a report on Queen Christina, Pierre-Hector Chanut, the French Minister to Sweden, described the odd way she behaved with her woman companions:

"... The way she occupied herself indoors differed so much from the things her ladies talked about, that she rarely addressed them, and then only on one particular topic. . . . She left them alone on one side of her room and went over to talk with the gentlemen, the subjects of her conversation being serious ones of course. She always paid gracious attention to any among them who suggested themes which she thought useful to discuss. But if there were persons whose limitations she knew and from whom she thought she could learn little, she cut the conversation off and continued the talk not a moment longer than was necessary."

French philosopher and scientist, came to Stockholm to teach her philosophy. But he could not endure the rigors of the northern climate and died there within a year.

In the late 1640s, revolutions broke out in western Europe. The English monarchy was overthrown and Charles I executed. In Paris a rebellion nearly ended the French monarchy. Such extraordinary events alarmed every ruler. Oxenstierna worried about popular protest in Sweden over the high taxes levied for the military and for the extravagant display of the court. In 1650 a poor harvest caused widespread hunger. The peasants grumbled over the high price of food, angered by the way the aristocracy flaunted its power and privileges. What had ordinary Swedes gotten out of military adventures abroad?

Although Sweden was an absolute monarchy, the people through their Assembly still had some means to have their views considered. To conciliate the people, Oxenstierna asked Christina to limit her large expenditures on art, architecture, and music. She resented the attempt at constraint and defied him by giving large grants of crown lands to returning war veterans and by bestowing titles, lands, and money on her favorites. She showed no interest in or grasp of finance.

Still, on the whole her reign was beneficial. She backed the publication of Sweden's first newspaper and the first nationwide school law. Oxenstierna had described Sweden's province in Finland as hopelessly backward: "There is no culture, the inhabitants are beasts," he said. He and Christina held that one of the main tasks of government was to "civilize our nation." For this educational work the Protestant clergy was assigned a specially important role.

Christina granted new powers to the towns and encouraged the development of mining, trade, and manufacturing. And naturally, she continued her generous support of science and the arts.

Every monarchy was concerned about the succession to the throne. Whom would Christina marry? Would he be an asset to Sweden or a political disaster? The young queen pretended she loved her cousin Charles, who was exactly her age, but it was apparently a tactic to calm worries about who would succeed her if she had no child to take the throne. Privately, as we saw, she confided she had no desire to marry. Perhaps too she feared that once married, she would lose some of her power to her husband.

Growing weary of her royal obligations, Christina decided she'd had enough. She wanted to shed the heavy cares of state and enjoy personal freedom. In 1651 she announced she would abdicate. Oxenstierna was shocked and her council disapproved, so she delayed taking this action for a time. But in 1654, at the age of twenty-eight, she insisted, and this time she carried it out. She designated her cousin, Charles X, as her heir.

That June, after twenty-two years as monarch, she left Sweden, assured of a lifetime income from her Swedish landholdings. She went first to the Netherlands and then to Austria. There she openly announced her conversion to Roman Catholicism, a religion forbidden in Sweden. To most Swedes, this was an appalling betrayal. For thirty years, Lutheran Sweden had been fighting bitter wars against the Catholic powers. So this conversion seemed to come not so much out of personal beliefs but as a declaration of allegiance to the enemy.

I shall never be virtuous enough to be a saint, nor infamous enough to pretend to be one," Christina once said. She never lost interest in worldly affairs. Intellectual that she was, she was not above gossip. Once, when living for a time in Germany, she wrote a friend in Rome, begging him to send her all the dirt. "Tell me about cardinals, masquerades, balls, hunts, intrigues, love affairs, who's in, who's out. . . . I want to know it all, and at once."

Historians have argued for centuries over Christina's motives for conversion. In a fragment of autobiography she wrote: "I did not believe in the religion in which I was brought up. . . . When I grew older I made a kind of religion for myself." As queen, she was tolerant, wanting to safeguard religious freedom for all. Developing a friendship with a Catholic diplomat assigned to Stockholm, she learned about that church's doctrines. In her autobiography she wrote that when quite young, she had once said to her tutor, "How beautiful this religion is. I should like to belong to it." That the Catholic church respected celibacy aroused her interest. Her own attachment to celibacy, she said, "gave the first impulse" to her "honorable change of religion."

From Austria, Christina moved to Rome. Why Italy? She had wished to visit the country for a long time, admiring its art and music in her youth. As queen, she had invited an Italian opera company to perform in Stockholm. Her image of Italy was shaped by the ravishing music of its composers and the sensuous canvases and sculpture of its artists, so challenging to Swedish taste.

But surely the most important reason she went to Rome was that here only the pope took precedence over her. In any other place in Europe she would have had to subordinate herself to a king or a prince.

In December of 1655, Christina was welcomed to Rome by Pope Alexander VII. Soon, however, he was disillusioned with the famous convert. Her ways were too independent, too self-centered. She shunned public displays of piety. But by her personality and

Rome from a window

high style of living she created a sensation in Rome. She made her home in one princely palace or another and entertained lavishly. Quickly she became the center of a salon. Noblemen, cardinals, and intellectuals gathered there. Aware that she was the most prominent convert of the century, she suggested to other European monarchs of the Protestant faith that if they followed her example such conversions would end the religious wars that had divided the continent for the last 150 years. No one took her advice.

In Rome, Christina became a close friend and patron of Giovanni Bernini (1598–1680), the dominant figure of the Italian baroque period. He designed churches, fountains, monuments, tombs, and statues, and was the architect of St. Peter's Cathedral. His was an exuberant style, one that produced spectacular visual effects. He was also a great wit who wrote comedies. He had a very high opinion of Christina's judgment in art, saying she was one of the very few women who could appreciate what he created, "down to the most delicate touches."

Christina spent extravagantly on acquiring great paintings—works by Titian, Tintoretto, Raphael, Veronese, del Sarto, Correggio—and displaying them in her palace galleries. She furnished her rooms elegantly and spared no expense in providing her frequent guests with the finest foods and wines. In her library was a collection of manuscripts rated as one of the best in the world. She also acquired many valuable works of art from antiquity—sculpture, pictures, tapestries. Her collections of rare coins, medals, cameos, and gems were famous. Her palace gardens were like great parks, with magnificent trees and flower beds.

She not only followed Italy's current archeological excavations, but financed some of them herself, putting archaeologists and curators on her payroll.

Composers she admired, such as Alessandro Scarlatti, were often employed by Christina. Scarlatti wrote over a hundred operas and some 700 chamber cantatas. She offered concerts in her palace and took voice lessons herself, giving several hours of an evening to working with a singing master. But hers was a small mezzo-soprano voice, never good enough for the public to enjoy. Despite Christina's love for music, singers and musicians complained that she would chat loudly or even read a book during their performances. The audience grew so angry at times that they hissed her.

Not content with studying by herself, Christina founded two academies to bring together theologians, composers, poets, philosophers, scholars, and Rome's aristocrats. She liked to launch discussions of ethical and scientific questions—but within limits. Controversial issues raised by Galileo (1564–1642), the great

Italian astronomer, mathematician, and physicist, some of whose scientific find-ings had defied church views, were still taboo. Galileo concluded that the sun was the central body of the solar system; the earth was only a moving body revolv-ing with the other planets around the sun. This notion was considered dangerous to the Christian faith because it was contrary to the teachings of the church.

In her palace Christina built an observatory, employing two full-time astron-omers, and then added a research laboratory. She encouraged scholars in the humanities too; several dedicated their works to her. But like other intellectuals of her time, Christina could be a patron of charlatans as well as of scientists. Once she hired a Danish alchemist who said he could manufacture gold for her.

In the late 1670s, Christina was obliged to cut back on her support of the arts. She was running short of money. The income from her Swedish estates, on which she had counted, had been reduced. Refusing to charge admission to her own the-ater—that would be commercial!—she closed it down. Still, she managed to pro-duce operas in Bernini's little theater, or in a boys' school.

Then, in 1685, she celebrated the crowning of the Catholic King James II in England. She paid for a cantata to be written, which was performed by over a hundred singers lent by the pope, with an orchestra of 150 strings conducted by Corelli. The unprecedented magnificence of this musical mammoth dazzled Rome.

Although a supreme egotist, Christina still found room in her heart for others. She was known for her militant defense of personal freedoms, for her charities, and as a protector of the Jews in Rome. Conscious as she was of royal rank, Christina believed that people of talent deserved greater consideration than people who happened to be highborn. In her mind, artists were the true aristocracy. Her father had been no bigot, and neither was she. She believed in religious freedom, and when Louis XIV tried to force the French Protestants to forsake their faith, she had the courage to criticize him publicly for his brutality. Her complete lack of religious or racial prejudice was very rare for her time. She treated Jews just like Gentiles, even going out of her way to be courteous to Jews and to show them favor.

For the last thirty years of her life, Christina occupied a strange position: a talented queen without a realm. She died in 1689, at the age of sixty-three. Despite her differences at times with the four popes she had lived under, the eminent convert was given the final honor—burial in St. Peter's Cathedral.

Maria Theresa

1717 - 1780

Imagine being a mother with sixteen children to raise—and all the while governing an empire that covered one-third the surface of Europe! (Which task was harder?)

That was Maria Theresa, empress of Austria. She was a key figure in the power politics of eighteenth-century Europe. In the long line of monarchs called the Hapsburg dynasty, she was one of the most capable. And the most human of them all.

Today Austria is a small country. In the eighteenth century Austria was a vast collection of ill-matched lands—dukedoms, principalities, provinces in all parts of Europe—that had been patched into an empire by war or marriage. Vienna, the capital, sat at the heart of Europe. The kings and nobles of around that time had erected nearly three hundred palaces in the city. The court was the center of life amid this baroque splendor. The narrow streets of Vienna were crowded with thousands of horse-drawn carriages and coaches and wagons. Among the huge crowds out walking, you could see the colorful display of national costumes, mostly of southeastern Europe and Turkey.

Maria Theresa came to the throne at the age of twenty-three. Her father, Emperor Charles VI, who died leaving no male heir, had arranged for his eldest daughter to inherit the crown. She was poorly prepared for so heavy a burden. She grew up sheltered in royal palaces, educated by a strict governess Maria Theresa called the "she-fox." More emphasis was put on manners than on history. To the end of her reign, Maria Theresa would rarely read a book, and she never learned to spell correctly. As a child, she never gave any thought to politics.

Music—that was her passion, and indeed, all Vienna's. Everyone and everything made music. When the young princess sat down on a certain chair, it played a flute solo. Instead of chiming when the hours struck, clocks played melodies.

carriage ride

In the palace, elaborate operas were staged. At the age of six the little princess pranced onto the stage and warbled a solo before a delighted audience.

In 1723, the year Maria Theresa was six, the royal family made a trip to Prague, then a major city in the empire. Up front among the four hundred coaches streaming along the road was a special little one designed to show off Maria Theresa to the cheering crowds.

During their long stay in Prague, Maria Theresa's eye fell on handsome young Franz Stephan, heir to the duchy of Lorraine. The six-year-old girl fell madly in love with the fourteen-year-old boy. Already she knew that the marriages of royalty were arranged not for love, but for political advantage. But she would have no one else but Franz Stephan. All the royal families of Europe fought for years over who should get to marry Maria Theresa, but in the end, she had her way. The beautiful couple were wed in February 1736, when she was nineteen. In the first four years of marriage, she had three children, all girls.

And then, in the autumn of 1740, Emperor Charles died, and Maria Theresa became empress. Her father's death provided an excuse for other royals to try to seize Austrian lands. Austria's tired old ministers sneered at the notion that this "pretty young thing" could take charge of anything, much less an empire, and especially one threatened by invading armies. At this time pregnant with a fifth child, Maria Theresa was devastated as two of her living children died within months of each other. Leaping for the kill, Frederick the Great's troops marched into the Austrian province of Silesia and added it to his native Prussia. Other powers—France and Bavaria—prepared to tear their own big chunks out of what they believed to be a tottering empire.

But like everyone else, they were amazed by the extraordinary courage and strength of the young empress. She seemed to learn overnight how to command. She threw herself into the work of governing as if by instinct—consulting, negotiating, planning, dictating, holding the shaky empire together by force of will.

In the summer of 1741, the Bavarians began to move on Austria, with a French army heading east to join them. The empress had to rely on local princes when troops were needed. Now she appealed to reluctant Hungarian nobles for military aid. Unable to resist her passionate plea, they voted her six regiments. With them she drove the Bavarians out and made peace with the French. Two more wars, from which she suffered losses, would disrupt her reign, although Hapsburg power survived.

Despite all these troubles, Maria Theresa was able to devote her best energies to her great goals: the unification of her multilingual empire, and the reform of its outworn political and social system.

Her husband, Franz, had a nominal share in governing the Austrian provinces, but the real authority was always in her hands. He proved a poor military leader and was content to take a backseat. Although her love for him never faded, he turned out to be a womanizer, notorious for his numerous affairs. In Europe's court circles, this was nothing unusual. Husbands and wives often played a game of musical beds.

Although Maria Theresa was a woman ruling the most complex empire in all of Europe—made up of many different national and ethnic groups, each speaking its own language—she often said she believed a woman's place was in the home. Then what was she doing on the throne? "I am only here," she said, "because it is the will of God, and it is my duty." Yet her "feminine side" did not lack for outlets. In her dealing with her own people and with foreign powers she showed great tact, compassion, and understanding—qualities often thought of as feminine. No wonder her generals and her ministers were so loyal.

Her warmth, her lack of pretense, and her joy in life captivated all. She wore masks and joked at carnival time, rode horseback in the Vienna Woods, danced at balls, and laughed easily and often. She did away with formal court etiquette, welcomed the people to her audiences every morning, and encouraged them to speak freely.

Many legends about her sprang up. According to one, as Maria Theresa was walking in the palace gardens with her infant son Joseph and his nurse, they met a beggar woman holding a screaming baby to her dry breast. The empress paused to hand her a coin. But the woman angrily pushed it away, saying bitterly that gold would not quiet her hungry baby. Whereupon the empress took the baby in her arms and put it to her full breast.

Plainly she loved children. Once she said, "I am general and chief mother of my country." The portraits of the thirteen of her children who survived infancy show eight pretty girls in splendid lacy gowns and five handsome boys in periwigs and velvet breeches. Always there are puppy dogs somewhere in the painting. Sadly, she hadn't much time to spend with the children. She would drop by their classrooms when she could, but mostly she wrote messages to their tutors and governesses telling them exactly what she wanted them to teach and exactly how. The children were taught the three Rs, history, languages, geography, and religion, and got special instruction in dance and music. The whole family gathered together only on Sundays, for church and for dinner.

Even before her children entered their teens, Maria Theresa began calculating marriage plans. Each royal child was a great political asset. Through their marriages Austria could create alliances with old enemies or cement relations with traditional allies. Crown Prince Joseph, her eldest boy, was number one on her list. He was a willing student, slowly but stubbornly mastering knowledge, especially of the French Enlightenment thinkers, whose writings he loved. The Enlightenment—a powerful intellectual movement in eighteenth-century Europe and America—was shaped by the ideas and scientific discoveries of men like Sir Isaac Newton, René Descartes, Benedictus de Spinoza, Francis Bacon, and John Locke. Their con-

royal portrait

M a r i a

T h e r e s a

fidence in the power of human reason influenced many in their generation and in generations to come. They wanted no one to dictate what people should think. They opposed intolerance, censorship, and economic and social restraints. They believed that the enlightened government of a state could help bring about freedom and progress.

Joseph was shy with women, and not an easy talker. Luckily the bride his parents chose for him—Princess Isabella of Parma, a granddaughter of the king of France—was both beautiful and brilliant. He fell deeply in love with her, and she with him. They married in 1760.

It was Maria Theresa who pulled Austria out of its almost feudal way of life and pushed it into the modern world. She was a great reformer. She borrowed ideas from any source, even from Frederick the Great of Prussia, whom she hated. Before her time, Austria was not a highly organized empire. There were many dominions, each with its own administration and laws. Even the most basic of any government's needs—finances—were so poorly accounted for that no one knew how much money there was, where it came from, or how it was spent. Maria Theresa set up an advisory economic council and an auditing system to control finances.

Nor did anyone know the population of Austria. In 1771 the empress organized the first census and had the land surveyed as well. According to the census, the empire's people numbered 18 million. The empire covered one-third the surface of Europe.

Austria's economy was overwhelmingly agricultural. The men and women who labored on the land were serfs, bound to the nobles who owned the land. Their obligations to their masters were not defined by law; the overlords could do just about anything they liked to the peasants. The empress did not abolish serfdom, but she codified the obligations and services of both peasant and noble. Peasants, she insisted, must be allowed to acquire money to improve their condition. She allowed them to trade freely on the market the products they raised or created by hand. Thus they could earn cash to buy other things they might need or want.

Famine due to wars and crop failures was an ever-present threat in the eighteenth century. Maria Theresa introduced the potato as a new staple food, imitating what other European powers were doing with this wonderfully nutritious plant that had found its way across the ocean from Peru, where the Incas had grown it for centuries. Everywhere it provided a safeguard against starvation.

The empress ended the traditional tax-free status of the nobility and the clergy. Now they too had to pay property and income taxes, sharing the cost of government and social services. Trade within the empire and beyond its borders was encouraged by lowering tariff barriers and revising the system of payments on products imported into or exported from the country. The empress invited foreign business in to help develop nonagricultural resources such as minerals and

And however much I love my family and my children, so much that I would not spare myself effort, trouble, anxiety, or work, yet I would have preferred to them the country's general good if I had been persuaded in my conscience that I could further it, or that the well-being of my subjects required it, seeing that I am the general and chief mother of my country." —Maria Theresa timber. More industry would strengthen the empire and provide jobs. Maria Theresa even established a school of mining, turning out engineers and technicians. Social legislation to protect workers was adopted, and child labor was ended. She built Austria's first public housing project, close to factories.

The empress gradually changed the monetary system too. She had new currency made—at first the thaler, a silver coin, and then paper money also. To raise money she organized lotteries.

The military—the power upon which any state rests—was a mess. The officer corps had little training, poor weaponry, low pay, and no prestige. Not even the uniforms were standardized. In battle no one could tell friend from foe. Maria Theresa founded a military academy, created medals to honor victory and bravery, forbade the flogging of soldiers, and provided better care for and aid to disabled veterans. She increased her standing army to over 100,000 troops.

Without a decent system of education, little improvement could be expected in any aspect of life. Maria Theresa ordered the establishment of compulsory schooling at every level, and in every locality. For the first time schools would be paid for by the state. The three Rs would be taught in all villages, for she wanted the common people, not just the upper class, to be educated. Schooling, she said, is not a gift or a privilege; it is a human right. She made reforms in the universities too, taking them out of the hands of the church. She started teachers colleges and a medical school.

A pious and dedicated Catholic, Maria Theresa was concerned about the loose morals of those in her court and the nobility. Not to mention her husband! In 1747 she set up a Chastity Commission to regulate the morals of society. She meant to enforce virtue in public and private. A force of Chastity Police was chosen to ferret out hidden vice. They were stationed in theaters and ballrooms and patrolled the streets with orders to arrest girls found walking alone. At Austria's borders they ransacked the luggage of travelers, looking for "dirty" literature. They followed up on the complaints of jealous wives and jealous husbands. It all had little effect on people's behavior, except to make sin a subject for laughter.

Worth noting is the glorious music of Austria in the time of Maria Theresa.

Several of the greatest composers enriched the empire's culture. Vienna and other cities enjoyed the works of Franz Joseph Haydn, Wolfgang Amadeus Mozart, Ludwig van Beethoven, and many others. Mozart, born in 1756, was presented at the imperial court as a child virtuoso. At the age of six he performed his first composition there, his Minuet and Trio in G, for the empress. When the uninhibited little boy rose from the keyboard, he jumped on the lap of the empress, to the horror of the court. But she only laughed.

It was a kind of semi-private musical life. Until late in the eighteenth century, most performances were not given for a public that paid admission. Instead, counts and dukes paid composers a salary to write music, hire musicians, and conduct performances for small invited audiences. Even a Mozart was treated like one of the servants. Maria Theresa once referred to the Mozart family as "riffraff."

The snobbish aristocrats had healthy incomes from their vast estates as well as other sources. They were the basis of the great flowering of culture in that period. Yet the nobility accounted for only 2 to 3 percent of the population. Over 90 percent of the people lived in poverty.

Whether you were rich or poor, death was never absent from any eighteenth-century household. Even a monarch's. The 1760s were a terribly bad time for

Mozart

Maria Theresa's family. Isabella, Joseph's beloved wife, died of the smallpox at twenty-one, three years after their marriage. "I hardly know if I am still alive," the grieving Joseph wrote to his father-in-law. "I shall be unhappy all the rest of my days." Reluctantly, under great pressure from his mother, who wanted him to produce a male heir, he remarried. This time to Josepha, a sickly Bavarian princess. She too died of smallpox within two years. So did two of Maria Theresa's children, a boy of sixteen and a girl of twelve.

And as if all this grief were not already too much to bear, in 1765 Maria Theresa's husband, Franz, suddenly collapsed and died. The empress was only forty-eight, in the prime of life, but she never stopped mourning her husband's death. She cut off her pale gold ringlets, donned a black crepe cap, and moved into black-draped rooms in the palace. She never wore her jewels again, never danced again, never looked at another man.

Now her son Joseph became Emperor Joseph II, and his mother, the dowager empress. He too never remarried after losing Josepha. Mother and son had a running conflict over policy until her death fifteen years later. His adoption of the ideas of the French Enlightenment frightened her. Joseph admired the innovations of Frederick the Great, whom she detested. Her son wanted to go much further in reform than she did. Although in her codification of criminal and civil law, she had declared sorcery not to be a crime, she permitted the practice of torture to extract confessions. Joseph stopped it as one of his reforms. At the same time he repealed the death penalty, believing it to be no deterrent to crime. But he replaced it with lifelong hard labor, from which few survived more than a year.

Although her attitudes were modern in many ways, Maria Theresa was intolerant in religious matters. She had what historians called a "bitter loathing" for Jews. Her anti-Semitism was shared by many of her officials, but the educated middle class and nobility were somewhat more enlightened and liberal, or at least more pragmatic and reasonable. Until Joseph II changed her policy, Jews were persecuted in all kinds of ways. They paid much higher taxes; had to wear special clothing with a yellow patch; were shut within their homes on Christian holidays; were forbidden entrance to public taverns, theaters, and concerts; and were restricted in trade and industry.

Roman Catholicism was the faith of almost all Austrians, and religion was still the great dividing line in that century. Many Jews were tempted to be baptized into the Christian faith, the only way to overcome great hardship and disrespect. But even those who converted often felt themselves an oppressed minority, tolerated only within narrow limits. Some Austrians, however, like Mozart, treated Jews as equals. Free of social prejudices, Mozart counted many Jews among his neighbors, friends, and acquaintances. After the death of the empress, Joseph II lifted some of the restrictions on Jews. He allowed them into what had once been forbidden professions, as well as into the army.

Maria Theresa, of course, was neither a freethinker nor a democrat. Like most monarchs, she wished to strengthen and centralize her power. She did not want to be answerable to any other institution, including the Church of Rome. With that aim in mind, she and her son Joseph forced the church to stop intervening in the affairs of government. They wanted the church to serve national interests, and its clergymen to be subject to the state. A year after his mother's death, Joseph would proclaim total religious freedom and forbid curtailment of civil liberties on religious grounds.

By the mid-1770s the empress had grown enormously stout, and her health began to fail. Giving over most of the royal functions to Joseph, she retired to the beautiful baroque palace of Schönbrunn, which she built on the outskirts of Vienna. In November 1780, she died.

Catherine the Great

1729 - 1796

Only a few women have given their names to a period of history. Catherine the Great was one of those legendary figures. Her name marks a major epoch in the development of the multinational Russian empire. She was the all-powerful empress of its vast domain for nearly thirty-five years.

In her long career on the throne she confronted one crisis after another and managed them so well that even today she enjoys an immense reputation, not only in Russia but worldwide.

Catherine's life was full of odd twists and turns. For one thing, she was not Russian. She was born in 1729 as Princess Sophia, the daughter of a minor German prince and a noblewoman. Even when she was a little girl "this idea of a crown began running in my head like a tune," she said later. She saw her father "very seldom," and her mother "did not bother much about me."

In aristocratic circles a woman's value was linked to her beauty. Little Sophia was pleasing, though plain, and would "chatter on boldly and endlessly" when with grown-ups. But so striking was her intelligence that she was petted and complimented by everyone. "I heard it said so often that I was smart, that I really believed it." Yet her mother thought homely girls did not find husbands. Would her Sophie end up in a convent, boarding with nuns?

studying

Not if Sophie could help it! She had her own opinions on everything, and during a time when most girls were expected to be obedient, she resisted being ordered about. She studied German, French, and religion; learned history and geography; loved music, dancing, and reading. Big for her age and strong, she enjoyed playing the rough-and-tumble games boys liked.

An important influence on Sophie was her brilliant French governess, Babette Cardel. She helped Sophie pierce through the fog of superstition that smothered thinking in that time. Use your common sense, she told Sophie; accept nothing on faith. She nourished Sophie's independence of mind and passed on to the young girl new ideas about social equality and political reform.

As Sophie grew older, she impressed people with her original turn of mind. Mama began to think her daughter might after all make a good bargain on the royal bride market.

She was right. Political matchmakers went to work, and at the age of fourteen, Sophie was chosen to be the wife of Grand Duke Peter, then only fifteen, heir to the throne of Russia. In 1744, Sophie arrived in Russia, converted from the Lutheran faith of her homeland to the Russian Orthodox church, and took the title Grand Duchess Catherine, her name from then on. She married Peter the following year.

At that time Russia was ruled by Empress Elizabeth, a daughter of Peter the Great. Catherine set herself to studying the behavior and tastes of the imperial court. She learned who the influential people were and what they were like. The empress, then thirty-four, was a handsome and vain woman, much relieved to find Catherine would not rival her in looks.

As head of state, the empress was always in fear of plots to overthrow or assassinate her. Her court was full of schemers, people whose loyalty could be bought and officials she could not rely on. Elizabeth looked to the much-feared secret police to spy on people's behavior and nip any plots in the bud.

Elizabeth herself had refused to make a political marriage. Instead, she married for love, a secret marriage to a handsome Ukrainian singer, a commoner who cared nothing for politics, only for music. Childless, the empress decreed her throne would go to her nephew Peter, and then to any children he and Catherine might have.

Peter proved a great disappointment. He had no political sense, telling everyone that he favored Germany far above Russia and that Russians were vastly inferior to Germans. The grandson of Peter the Great (1672–1725), Peter was nothing like his powerful and brilliant ancestor. His grandfather Peter the Great, by ruthless reforms and the adoption of Western military and industrial techniques, had begun the long process of transforming medieval Russia into a modern imperial power. A year older than Catherine, the young Peter behaved like a spoiled child with a nasty temper. Although not stupid, he resisted learning anything from his tutors. He drank too much and liked nothing more than playing military games. Theirs was a miserable marriage.

Catherine lived in a society where women counted for little, in her husband's eyes as well as in all Russia's. Not so long ago, before the time of Peter the Great's reforms, women were confined to their own quarters, kept apart from anyone but relatives. The higher in society a woman was, the more thoroughly she was isolated. Only the poor peasant women, whose labor was essential to the family and whose poverty did not permit their segregation, mixed freely with men.

Not only custom, but the law virtually enslaved women to their fathers and husbands. They faced terrible punishment if they disobeyed their masters. As a Russian proverb put it, "The wife is in the power of her husband." Catherine's husband was raised to believe a few punches to a wife's head now and then were good for the marriage. Mild punishment, when you consider that some husbands in those days hung their wives by the hair, stripped them naked, and beat them until their flesh was torn and their bones broken.

Although many women died under such brutality, Russian law did not hold their husbands guilty of any crime. But if a wife killed her tormentor, the law called for her to be buried up to her neck in a pit and left to die of thirst, an agony that could last seven or eight days. Common too was the sight of women whose noses had been cut off because they had offended their husbands. Some wives ran away from their abusive husbands. If caught, they were stuck in a convent, dead to the world outside.

Disappointed by her husband's silly and childish behavior, Catherine decided to survive by humoring him. She acted like his loyal friend, "tried to be as charming as possible to everyone, and was pleased when I realized that I was daily winning the affection of the public." She decided to make Russian ways her own and to master the language, so while everyone else slept, she would jump out of bed in the middle of the night and "learn by heart all the lessons." But studying was not all she did. She proved to be a superb rider and hunter, spending sometimes twelve hours in the saddle.

The young husband showed her no affection. He bragged to Catherine about his sexual adventures (some think these were imaginary) with other women. Desperately lonely, she sought love outside her marriage. She seems to have had a series of lovers during the rest of her life. Some people called her immoral, though such behavior was common in court circles everywhere. In 1754, when she was twenty-five, Catherine's son Paul was born. Was his father Peter or Catherine's lover, Sergei Saltykov? Probably Sergei.

Avid for achieving power someday in her own right, Catherine continued to read "everything that came my way." It was unusual for anyone at the Russian court, let alone for a woman, to be interested in books. About half the aristocrats could barely read, and less than a third could write. Catherine studied the classical historians Plutarch and Tacitus, who taught her much about the ways of the rulers of ancient Rome. From reading Machiavelli she learned about the power struggles among the Renaissance princes of Italy. And the French writers of the Enlightenment like Voltaire and Diderot and Jean-Jacques Rousseau pointed her thinking in a radical direction. Theirs was a movement based on the idea that all people were entitled to certain basic rights (echoed soon in Thomas Jefferson's words "Life, Liberty, and the Pursuit of Happiness"). A government's duty, these writers said, was to develop sensible and practical means to improve the lives and protect the welfare of all its citizens. Not passion, but reason; not tradition, but logic, should govern decisions. Catherine was taking in theories about how to govern, and thinking about how to manage the difficult details of everyday administration in a country as vast and backward as Russia.

the classics

She knew right away that Peter was not capable of governing Russia. And quite soon, she saw the possibility of eliminating him and taking the throne herself. When Empress Elizabeth died early in 1762, Russia, allied with Austria and France, was fighting the Seven Years' War against Prussia. Peter, now crowned emperor, angered many powerful people by deserting his allies and signing a treaty of alliance with Prussia.

It only added to the hatred for him when it became clear that Peter wanted to get rid of Catherine and rule alone. But the court and the army supported his wife. Regiments in St. Petersburg rallied to Catherine's side and arrested Peter. He was forced to abdicate. Eight days later, he died, probably murdered by Catherine's supporters. In September 1762, at the age of thirty-three, she was crowned Catherine II, empress of Russia.

She was thoroughly "Russified" now, after eighteen years in her adopted country. And respected and admired by many. But she faced enormous problems: an empty treasury, huge state debts, an army unpaid for months, a largely ignorant and incompetent administration scattered over the wide land.

How to govern a land that stretched from the Polish frontier to the Pacific Ocean? Remember, there were no railroads then, no motor vehicles, no telegraph or telephone, no radio or television. People moved on foot or on horse, over terrible roads. Communication was painfully slow and difficult. Only the many river systems made travel and trade by boat a bit easier.

For so large a territory the population was tiny: only about 16 million in 1725. Even the biggest towns had relatively small populations. In the whole of the vast eastern region called Siberia, nearly 3 million square miles, there were only 400,000 people. The Russians were a mixed population ethnically—mostly Slavs, but several other groups too.

Like most European states at this time, Russia was an absolute monarchy. There were no limits to the ruler's will, no obstacles of a legal or social nature. The Russian czar or emperor was the sole source of law. True, there was now a

Senate (it had been introduced by Peter the Great), but it was not an elected body, only a small council of appointed officials whose job was to coordinate policy at home and abroad. Below the Senate were various departments responsible for commerce, the military, and so on.

Of great importance was the security service, the feared and hated political police. Its function was to ferret out any opposition to the ruler or his or her policies. Critical remarks, disrespectful words, nasty rumors repeated could lead to arrest, and often to torture, in order to force confession and the implication of others.

Taking power in Russia would seem a dim prospect for one with no experience in ruling. Yet the new empress had many assets: a fine mind, a hunger to learn, skill in judging others, an iron will, and incredible energy. Why couldn't she become the female Peter the Great? This was her chance to prove she could mold Russia into a prosperous and powerful state.

Catherine set about trying to change Russia. She would not hide in her palaces as other monarchs did, but go boldly before the people, plunging into every aspect of policy, as Peter the Great had done. But unlike Peter, she wanted to persuade her people to change their ways, not force them.

She picked a personal cabinet to give her advice and to transmit her plans to officials throughout the empire. She chose as her ministers men of great talent. Her policy would be to richly reward people who proved their loyalty. She handed out titles, promotions, money, landed estates, and the serfs who went with the land. She brought the sleepy Senate back to life, appointed new members, and berated them when they slipped back into the old ways of laziness and indifference. As she introduced reforms, she learned to deal with the inevitable factions within the court and her cabinet, representing conflicting interests and competing for favor.

But the Russian empire was enormous! How could authority be transmitted downward and outward to the most remote provinces with any expectation that, left to themselves, government officials would do just what the empress asked? Only centralized rule was suited to Russian conditions, Catherine believed. There had to be a chain of command from the center, radiating out to every region and locality, with severe punishment for those who failed to carry out orders.

Of course this was not a democratic government, as we understand it today. But then, nowhere in the world at that time would you find representative democracy functioning.

The records show Catherine was a practical administrator, intensely concerned with a multitude of government affairs. She worked much harder than most of her officials. Her habit was to get up about five or six A.M., put on informal dress, have coffee, and then keep four secretaries busy during a fifteen-hour day, writing out memoranda, orders, policy papers, letters. Yet she was still a warm human being, recognizing her own mistakes and able to laugh at them and herself.

She knew Russia badly needed a just and workable legal system. Unlike most European nations, Russia had no tradition of legal training. The laws were a chaotic mess. How to find a way out of it?

Catherine decided on a bold experiment. She summoned an assembly of some six hundred people elected from all regions and classes (except serfs and women). They met in Moscow in 1767. From this assembly Catherine hoped to hear what the people themselves believed Russia needed in the way of better government.

To guide discussion, in her own hand she wrote out what she called her *Great Instruction*. It outlined her own notion of ideal government. Her *Great Instruction* incorporated many of the ideas put forth by the Enlightenment thinkers of France, England, Germany, and Italy. It called for freedom of religion and dissent, opposed the use of torture, and declared that the land is best cultivated by those who are free and own their land.

Monarchs, Catherine said, "should do good and avoid doing evil as much as one reasonably can, out of love for humanity. . . . The laws must always remain sacred to monarchs, because they last forever while subjects and rulers disappear. . . . Men should be judged according to the law." And liberty? That, she said, is "the should of everything, without it all is dead. I want the law to be obeyed, but I want no slaves. I want the general aim of making people happy, but no caprice, no fantasies, no tyranny which might undermine it."

"I want no slaves." But what about the serfs? Would the legislative assembly do anything about them?

Even before Catherine gained the throne she was planning to emancipate the serfs. About 95 percent of Russia's economy was agricultural, and half the peasants were then serfs. They belonged to the landowners, who were usually nobles. Some nobles owned tens of thousands of serfs. Long after serfdom had disappeared from western Europe, it was still legal in Russia. Serfdom had much in common with slavery in America, except that there was no color line. Serfs were white-skinned. The church also had vast estates worked by serfs, who could not be sold or given away. And Catherine's own family held peasants in serfdom.

To get rid of serfdom she needed the support of the landowning class. But she saw that the masters would never agree to liberate the peasants, whose unpaid labor made them rich. Rather than throw the country into chaos or civil war, she decided to live with the evils of serfdom. Against her own expressed beliefs, she let the system continue and even expand. Like many other heads of state—in our time as well as hers—she was torn by conflicting forces, and sometimes sacrificed principle to retain power.

The assembly debated for almost a year but failed to produce even a single law on any subject. Legislative reform was too great a task to be hurried through. Nevertheless, the committee reports, the lists of grievances, and the proposed laws on the rights of nobles, townspeople, and peasants produced a vast amount of useful information about the needs and wishes of the people.

Catherine's noble experiment, while a failure, did much to enhance her reputation. Her *Great Instruction* was translated into almost every European language and was heavily publicized in journals and newspapers. She gained world celebrity as a philosopher-sovereign.

What finally shut down the assembly was the eruption of war between Russia and Turkey. No one could be sure the Russian soldiers would fight willingly for Catherine. Except Catherine herself. Typically superconfident, she had her army and navy boldy attack the Turkish forces by land and by sea. "My soldiers go to war against Turkey as if they were on their way to a wedding," she boasted. Her great victories fired up her people's nationalistic passion and made the empress an international heroine. Now the leading nations of Europe had to reckon with Russia. She was a Great Power, one to be feared and bargained with.

What impression did Catherine make around this time? The British ambassador to her court, Sir George Macartney, left his report:

Her air is commanding and full of dignity. . . . I never saw in my life a person whose port, manner, and behavior answered so strongly to the idea I had formed to myself of her. Tho' in the thirty-seventh year of her age she may still be called beautiful. Those who knew her younger say they never remembered her so lovely as at present, and I very readily believe it. . . . It is inconceivable with what address she mingles the ease of behavior with the dignity of her rank, with what facility she familiarizes herself with the meanest of her subjects, without losing a point of her authority, and with what astonishing magic she inspires at once both respect and affection. Her conversation is brilliant, perhaps too brilliant, for she loves to shine in conversation. She does so to an uncommon degree, and 'tis almost impossible to follow her, her sallies are so quick, so full of fire, spirit, and vivacity.

Russia under Catherine turned more and more toward Europe, acquiring superior technology from the West. Countless westerners were called in to help Russia. Engineers, architects, artisans, painters, musicians, and governesses flooded into the raw land, whose upper and middle classes—aristocrats, landlords, politicians, intellectuals—were eager to learn from them. But these classes made up only a small part of the population.

Most of the people were still untouched by positive change. And from time to time, unwilling to be oppressed any longer, they rebelled. One of the greatest revolts broke out in Catherine's regime in 1773. Emilian Pugachov, a former officer of Cossacks—peasant soldiers from certain parts of the Russian empire—began an uprising in the Ural region which spread rapidly through the vast southeastern provinces. Pugachov knew the people's discontents, their poverty, their hopes. He promised them a happier life after he overthrew Catherine and became emperor. At least 200,000—both Russian and non-Russian peoples of the empire—soldiers, workers, peasants, serfs—rallied to Pugachov's banners. His troops murdered government officials, slaughtered landowners and their families, burned down manor houses, seized money and grain, raped and looted. It was a war on the elite of the empire. By June 1774, Pugachov's troops were ready to march on Moscow. At that point the war with Turkey ended in a treaty and Catherine sent her best troops to crush the rebellion. Pugachov was defeated, captured, and beheaded.

With Turkey and Pugachov both overcome, Russia enjoyed peace for several years. Catherine proclaimed happier times were coming. To prove it, she repealed many taxes and proclaimed amnesty for those guilty of taking part in the Pugachov revolt as well as for army deserters, criminals who'd served ten years, and runaway state peasants.

In 1775, she and her advisers produced a new legal code meant to reorganize local government, making it somewhat more liberal, more effective, more responsible. Her reforms included new law courts, better policing, and a public welfare system. Medical services too were improved, in response to the tragic experience of recent mass epidemics. Even the penal system was modernized to a degree.

What Catherine achieved was limited by the realities of Russian life—not enough educated people, irresponsible officials, widespread illiteracy, the old tradition of favoritism and corruption. Nevertheless, she deserves credit for giving her society a legal framework, for improving the connection between all sections and the center of power, and for opening the way to further reforms.

Catherine realized that in order for Russia to progress, education had to be modernized and extended. In Russia, the Orthodox church educated only priests, not laypeople. There were no great state or private schools such as in western Europe. Moscow University had been founded only a few years before Catherine's reign began. Catherine opposed creating narrow, specialized, vocational  schools. She wanted a broad curriculum to create "new people" with a heightened sense of duty toward society and their fellow beings. Schools were started in the towns of each province, though not in the villages. These were free, coeducational, and open to all social classes (except that the children of serfs had to have their landlord's permission to attend). She launched teacher-training institutes, published textbooks, including her own *Primer for Youth*, and erected buildings. Although schooling was free, it was not compulsory. It was just a beginning, perhaps, with only 70,000 children attending state schools by the time Catherine died. Still, it *was* a beginning that others could carry forward.

Cultural life in all its aspects was also a great concern to Catherine. In absolute monarchies at that time, the arts were concentrated around the court. Catherine subsidized the theater, putting on plays by many great writers as a means of educating the public. She herself wrote plays in Russian that were presented and published anonymously. Choral and instrumental music was performed at court. Catherine wrote the librettos for a number of operas set to music by visiting composers from Italy or Spain as well as by Russians.

She subsidized the ballet as well, and built a private theater in the Hermitage Palace in St. Petersburg. She promoted public criticism of society's vices and defects by backing a satiric journal called *All Sorts of Things.* (She even wrote anonymously for it herself.) Other such periodicals soon sprang up, encouraged by the loosening of censorship. She never closed any of the critical press, though with such a small reading public, few endeavors lasted more than a year or two.

To bring Enlightenment ideas to Russians who could not read French or German, she subsidized the translation of foreign books. She herself loved to write and produced many literary works in Russian and some in French. She helped write the first dictionary of the Russian language. She corresponded eagerly and often with such great French thinkers as Voltaire, and gave generous support to Diderot for his creation of the immense *Encyclopédie.* At her invitation and expense, Diderot visited her in Russia for about six months, conversing with her almost daily about social and political questions.

The museum in the Hermitage Palace, visited today by people from everywhere because it houses one of the world's greatest art collections, was built by

Catherine as an addition to the Winter Palace. The museum contains a thousand rooms, displaying many of the finest works of the world's masters. This was one of the ways Catherine associated herself with the Enlightenment, with progress, with the arts.

She had a great influence too on Russian art and architecture. She followed trends in other countries and invited foreign artists to work in Russia. She sent Russian painters and architects to study abroad. Peter the Great had founded the splendid city of St. Petersburg on swamps, and she made the city even more beautiful. She commissioned one of the city's magnificent landmarks, the statue of Peter the Great (the "Bronze Horseman" of Pushkin's poem).

Catherine had begun her reign as a liberal reformer. Yet like many other rulers, she ended it as a bitter reactionary. In 1789, the French Revolution stunned the world. During it, King Louis XVI and his queen, Marie Antoinette, were executed. Catherine and all the crowned heads of Europe were terrified. The divine right of kings? Nonsense! The privileges of the aristocracy? Ended! Catherine, though once devoted to the Enlightenment, now feared its teachings might lead to her own downfall.

statue of Peter the Great

Another threat, closer to home, came when Poles began agitating for independence and a liberal constitution. Poland, an ancient kingdom long coveted by its three powerful neighbors—Russia, Prussia, and Austria—had recently been divided among these three, losing its independence. What Catherine had once thought good for Russia, she now called a revolutionary danger, and sent in troops to take control of a big part of the country. Worse was to come when Tadeusz Kościuszko, the Polish general who had served under George Washington in the American Revolution, led a national uprising in his homeland. Catherine's response was a savage assault upon Warsaw in which 20,000 men, women, and children were massacred. In 1795 she erased Poland from the map of Europe by dividing it up yet another time with Prussia and Austria. Earlier partitions of Poland, in 1772 and 1793, had brought more and more territory under Russian control. This was the final one, ending the independence of a great eastern European state.

On November 6, 1796, after a brief illness, Catherine died. Her son, Paul I, became emperor.

Historians seem to agree that perhaps 90 percent of the Russian people got few or no benefits from the many reforms Catherine introduced. Out of the profits of serfdom—the system of forced labor—came the funds to finance the great costs of the economic, cultural, and military projects the empress sponsored. She took much pride in those achievements. And perhaps she eased her conscience by telling herself that the blood and sweat extracted from the serfs, though it did them no good, had not been wasted.

Would you agree?

$\mathcal{R}$esearching the lives of people who lived thousands or even a few hundred years ago has many problems. The farther back in time you go, the fewer are the sources. Ancient sources on which inquiry has to be based are fragmentary. Little exists in writing. The historian has to look to nonliterary sources—coins, inscriptions, shrines, monuments, stela, reliefs. Much depends on archeological evidence, evidence that may be amended or wiped out by future digs. Even for medieval times the records are few, and the personalities to be constructed often only shadowy, insubstantial.

Given the scarcity of evidence in some cases, conclusions must be speculative. You have to say that there is much you do not know, and declare this is your best guess.

Even when you have what seems to be ample evidence—documents, letters, memoirs, diaries, autobiographies—it is often written by people with an ax to grind. They wish to make themselves or someone else look good—or bad! Remember too that until recently most history was written by the elite, the dominant ones. The miserable lives that made a queen's luxury possible were not recorded in history, except in the context of bloody acts of rebellion.

To judge public opinion of a queen is difficult under such circumstances. There were, until not long ago, few or no newspapers or periodicals. And what opinion could be found was often prejudiced or ill-informed. The historian or biographer has to sort out the probable from the unlikely, accepting whatever limits there are as he tries to get at the plain facts, and to understand them.

$\mathcal{T}$he sources used are arranged here by chapter. For more general information on historical periods, from various perspectives, I referred to many other works. Among these were:

Anderson, Bonnie S., and Judith P. Zinsser. *A History of Their Own: Women in Europe from Prehistory to the Present.* New York: Harper, 1989.

Barber, Elizabeth Wayland. *Women's Work: The First Two Thousand Years.* New York: Norton, 1994.

Braudel, Fernand. *A History of Civilizations.* New York: Penguin, 1993.

———. *The Wheels of Commerce: Civilization and Capitalism, Fifteenth to Eighteenth Century.* New York: Harper, 1982.

Commire, Anne, ed. *Historical World Leaders.* 4 vols. Detroit: Gale, 1994.

Dupuy, R. Ernest, and Trevor N. Dupuy. *The Harper Encyclopedia of Military History.* New York: HarperCollins, 1993.

Hale, John. *The Civilization of Europe in the Renaissance.* New York: Touchstone, 1993.

Knapton, Ernest John. *Europe: 1415-1815.* New York: Scribner's, 1958.

Lerner, Gerda. *The Creation of Feminist Consciousness: From the Middle Ages to 1870.* New York: Oxford University Press, 1994.

McNeill, William. *The Rise of the West: A History of the Human Community.* Chicago: University of Chicago Press, 1963.

Parry, J. H. *The Age of Reconnaissance.* Berkeley, CA: University of California Press, 1981.

Pomeroy, Sarah B. *Goddesses, Whores, Wives and Slaves: Women in Classical Antiquity.* New York: Schocken, 1975.

Reynolds, Robert. *Europe Emerges: 600–1750.* Madison: University of Wisconsin Press, 1967.

ESTHER

Ausubel, Nathan. *The Book of Jewish Knowledge.* New York: Crown, 1964.

Biale, David. *Power and Powerlessness in Jewish History.* New York: Schocken, 1986.

Book of Esther. Old Testament, King James Version.

Comay, Joan. *Who's Who in the Old Testament.* New York: Oxford University Press, 1993.

Steinsaltz, Adin. *Biblical Images: Men and Women of the Bible.* New York: Basic, 1984.

CLEOPATRA

Finley, M. R. *Politics in the Ancient World.* Cambridge, England: Cambridge University Press, 1983.

Fraser, Antonia. *Cleopatra: The Warrior Queen.* New York: Vintage, 1990.

Grant, Michael. *Cleopatra.* Lanham, MD: Barnes & Noble Books, 1995.

Hughes-Hallett, Lucy. *Cleopatra: Histories, Dreams, and Distortions.* New York: Harper, 1990.

James, T. G. H. *An Introduction to Ancient Egypt.* New York: Farrar, Straus, 1979.

Said, Edward. *Culture and Imperialism.* New York: Vintage, 1994.

BOUDICCA

Gibbon, Edward. *Decline and Fall of the Roman Empire.* New York: Viking, 1948.

Salway, Peter. *Roman Britain.* New York: Oxford University Press, 1981.

Scollard, H. H. *Roman Britain: Outpost of the Empire.* New York: Thames & Hudson, 1979.

ZENOBIA

Gibbon, Edward. *Decline and Fall of the Roman Empire.* New York: Viking, 1948.

Vaughan, Agnes Carr. *Zenobia of Palmyra.* New York: Doubleday, 1967.

ELEANOR

Cantor, Norman F. *Medieval Lives.* New York: HarperCollins, 1994.

Hallam, Elizabeth, ed. *The Plantagenet Chronicles.* Avenel, NJ: Crescent, 1995.

Holmes, Urban T., Jr., *Daily Living in the Twelfth Century.* Madison, WI: University of Wisconsin Press, 1964.

Kelly, Amy. *Eleanor of Aquitaine and the Four Kings.* Cambridge, MA: Harvard University Press, 1950.

Meade, Marion. *Eleanor of Aquitaine.* New York: Penguin, 1977.

Petit-Dutaillis, Charles. *The Feudal Monarchy in France and England.* New York: Harper, 1964.

Seward, Desmond. *Eleanor of Aquitaine: The Mother Queen.* Lanham, MD: Barnes & Noble Books, 1978.

Temko, Allan. *Notre-Dame of Paris: The Biography of a Cathedral.* New York: Viking, 1952.

ISABEL

Braudel, Fernand. *The Mediterranean in the Age of Philip II.* 2 vols. New York: Harper, 1973.

Grayzel, Solomon. *A History of the Jews.* Philadelphia, PA: Jewish Publication Society, 1947.

Liss, Peggy K. *Isabel the Queen: Her Life and Times.* New York: Oxford University Press, 1992.

Netanyahu, B. *The Origins of the Inquisition in Fifteenth-Century Spain.* New York: Random House, 1995.

Plaidy, Jean. *The Spanish Inquisition.* Lanham, MD: Barnes & Noble Books, 1994.

Rubin, Nancy. *Isabella of Castile: The First Renaissance Queen.* New York: St. Martin's Press, 1991.

ELIZABETH

Fraser, Antonia, ed. *The Lives of the Kings and Queens of England.* Berkeley, CA: University of California Press, 1975.

————. *The Warrior Queens.* New York: Vintage, 1990.

Hibbert, Christopher. *The Virgin Queen: Elizabeth I: Genius of the Golden Age.* Reading, MA: Addison-Wesley, 1991.

Jenkins, Elizabeth. *Elizabeth the Great.* New York: Coward McCann, 1959.

Rowse, A. L. *The England of Elizabeth.* Madison, WI: University of Wisconsin Press, 1978.

CHRISTINA

Barea, Ilsa. *Vienna.* New York: Alfred A. Knopf, 1966.

Elstob, Eric. *Sweden: A Political and Cultural History.* Lanham, MD: Rowman & Littlefield, 1979.

Masson, Georgina. *Queen Christina.* New York: Farrar, Straus, 1968.

Stolpe, Sven. *Christina of Sweden.* New York: Macmillan, 1966.

MARIA THERESA

Braunbehrens, Volkman. *Mozart in Vienna: 1781–1791.* New York: Harper, 1991.

Hoffman, Paul. *The Spell of the Vienna Woods.* New York: Holt, 1994.

Macartney, C. A. *The Habsburg Empire.* New York: Macmillan, 1969.

McGuigan, Dorothy Gies. *The Habsburgs.* New York: Doubleday, 1966.

Pick, Robert. *Empress Maria Theresa.* New York: Harper, 1966.

Stanka, Hugo, ed. *Not All About Austria.* Vienna, Austria: Young Austria, 1995.

CATHERINE

Alexander, John T. *Catherine the Great.* New York: Oxford University Press, 1989.

Erickson, Carolly. *Great Catherine.* New York: Crown, 1994.

Furbank, P. N. *Diderot: A Critical Biography.* New York: Alfred A. Knopf, 1992.

Madariaga, Isabel de. *Catherine the Great: A Short History.* New Haven, CN: Yale University Press, 1990.

134